Lawyers in the Making

norc

NATIONAL OPINION RESEARCH CENTER
MONOGRAPHS IN SOCIAL RESEARCH

*This book is a joint publication with the
American Bar Foundation*

Lawyers in the Making

By

SEYMOUR WARKOV

With a Chapter

By

JOSEPH ZELAN

Introduction

By

LOUIS A. TOEPFER

ALDINE PUBLISHING COMPANY
Chicago

*The research reported herein was supported
by the American Bar Foundation, the Law
School Admission Test Council, the Cooperative
Research Program of the Office of Education,
U.S. Department of Health, Education, and
Welfare, and Public Health Service
E Grant M5615 from the National
Institutes of Health*

*First published 1965 by
ALDINE Publishing Company
320 West Adams Street
Chicago, Illinois 60606*

*Library of Congress Catalog Card Number 65–26753
Designed by Greer Allen
Printed in the United States of America*

Preface

In the spring of 1961, the National Opinion Research Center collected self-administered questionnaires from a sample of 33,782 college seniors at 135 colleges and universities. This sample was designed to be representative of the graduates who would receive a bachelor's degree in June, 1961, from accredited and large non-accredited institutions throughout the country. The questionnaire (Appendix 1) included the following topics: intentions for graduate or professional study; application and acceptance status of those planning postgraduate study; expected financial sources including stipends; intended career field and type of employer; occupational values; academic performance and scholastic honors; background characteristics (religion, marital status, parental family characteristics, etc.); and others.

One year later, NORC followed up the entire sample and received mail questionnaires from 28,713 respondents. In the second questionnaire (Appendix 2) the respondents described their academic and employment circumstances during the academic year 1961–62, including the sources and kinds of financial assistance that had supported their graduate study and the plans they had made for further graduate or professional study. Thus the follow-up survey was able to determine to what extent the plans and expectations of the graduating college seniors in the spring of 1961 were fulfilled.

The data are of unprecedented scope and afford an opportunity for detailed analysis of the factors that influence the choice of a career field (Greeley, 1963; Miller, 1963; Davis, 1964, 1965). This monograph concerns those 1961 June graduates who planned to enter the field of law. Materials taken from the first survey make it possible to describe respondents' orientations to law at the time of graduation from college and, retrospectively, at the time they entered college as freshmen. It could be determined from the follow-up survey how many of the graduating seniors committed to a legal career actually entered a law school during the twelve-month period after completion of undergraduate work.

In addition to the question of recruitment to American law schools, Dr. Warkov considers the allocation of prospective law students to law schools. Because these schools display striking variation in quality as indicated by levels of ability among students, much of the analysis is concerned with an assessment of factors that account for the distribution of law students and the impact that exposure to a given kind of law school will have on students' reactions to legal study and plans for professional employment.

The report takes the form of a natural history of an embryonic legal career, beginning with career decisions during college, going through the first year of legal study, and ending with plans for remaining professional study. In Chapter 1 the comparative college freshman and graduating senior preferences for law are described. Recruitment is considered in Chapter 2: How many students reporting a senior-year preference for a career in law actually initiated professional study, and what are their personal, social, and academic characteristics? Chapter 3 considers the influence of occupational inheritance, i.e., lawyer fathers, on the career choice of graduating seniors. Chapter 4 analyzes the problem of allocation and the determinants of entry to top national law schools, intermediate law schools of solid reputation but not necessarily national or top quality, and other law schools. Chapter 5 considers the experience of the first year of law study in terms of reactions to course work, etc., and the single and joint effects of type of law school and the academic and social attributes of students on study patterns. In Chapter 6 materials are presented on the availability of stipends for law students and on certain academic and financial differences among stipend holders and other law students. Chapter 7 is devoted to continuity of legal study and the institutional and social correlates of preference for certain organizational settings in which lawyers undertake their professional practice.

While Dr. Warkov is solely responsible for writing the report on which this monograph is based, it is appropriate at this point to acknowledge the assistance of a number of persons on the staff of

NORC. Joseph Zelan was indispensable in moving the study to the stage where a draft could be prepared, and he is the author of the chapter in this volume on occupational inheritance. Others who were helpful in preparing the tables presented in the report include Bruce Frisbie, Dorothy Pownall, and Mrs. Carolyn Underhill. Mrs. Eleanor Nicholson did valuable editorial work on the report, and Mrs. Nella Siefert typed the text and the tables with her usual expertness.

NORC wishes to thank the members of the Advisory Committee of the American Bar Foundation, with whom the author met several times during his research and writing: Louis A. Toepfer, Chairman; Peter H. Holme, Jr.; Jo Desha Lucas; Roy L. Steinheimer; Malcolm D. Talbott; and Bethuel M. Webster. Geoffrey C. Hazard, Jr., Administrator, American Bar Foundation, offered valuable editorial advice; and John C. Leary, Deputy Administrator and Librarian, American Bar Foundation, expedited completion of the research.

One further acknowledgment should be made. The Law School Admission Test scores were made available for this study thanks to the efforts of Vice-Dean Louis A. Toepfer, of Harvard University Law School, and Dr. John A. Winterbottom, Program Director, Professional Examinations, Educational Testing Service.

Portions of Chapters 4 and 5 were presented at the 1963 meetings of the American Sociological Association (Los Angeles, August, 1963) and at the Annual Institute for Pre-Law Advisors and Law School Officials (Boston College Law School, December 7, 1963). Chapter 4 has also appeared in slightly different form in *The School Review* (Vol. 73, pp. 144–55).

This monograph was originally published in somewhat different form by the National Opinion Research Center as Report No. 96 (December, 1962).

NORMAN M. BRADBURN
Acting Director
National Opinion Research Center

Contents

List of Tables

List of Tables

List of Tables

Introduction

"On the whole they came by default," said Mr. Justice Frankfurter, writing about the law students whom he had known and why they studied law. And this is about as much as has ever been said concerning the "who and why" of law study.

It is puzzling that the legal profession and the law schools have given so little attention to understanding the sources upon which their future depends. Although much concern is now devoted to the public's attitude about lawyers and to how the layman chooses his attorney, little attention is being focused on how and why some young people choose the law for their career. Vague notions, old myths, and thought-shrugging generalizations are all we have to describe the raw material from which our lawyers come.

This is a study that was intended to throw light upon some of the darkness surrounding the conceptions of new lawyers. That it gives a better understanding of career choice in law is without question. But although it clears away some of the shadows in which our prospective lawyers have been obscured, hard questions about the profession emerge from its findings. Is the legal profession an anachronistic aristocracy? Why do religious differences have such a profound influence upon the origins, attitudes, and expectations of new lawyers? Why do economic differences play so great a role in their hopes and aspirations? Why does a random example of 1,800 law-inclined students include so few Negroes that they cannot be systematically studied? What are the consequences of having the law schools stand far below and behind the other graduate schools in the financial help which they offer to their students? It is in a way a tribute to this work that these questions emerge, for this study was meant to give no more than a limited look at the profession as it is mirrored in the eyes of prospective members.

These are turbulent times for the legal profession. One source of difficulty is that young lawyers are in such short supply. For every million people in the country, we are producing only about fifty new lawyers each year. As our population increases, our economy grows in complexity, our social order becomes more intricate, our government more active, and our people more sensitive. These changes generate an increasing need for lawyers far above the demands of yesteryear. The protection of the accused, the control of delinquency, the regulation of the metropolis, the congestion of courts, the economy of abundance, and the abolition of unfair advantages are only some of the problems which cry for help. But while these needs for lawyers are growing sharply, the profession has been growing slowly. In order to meet the challenges ahead, there must be an acceleration in the rate of growth. Young people must be recruited for the law in ever increasing numbers. And they must be somewhat special, for the law demands a high order of intelligence, character, industry, and judgment. It is from the top talent that the profession must draw new blood.

Although the colleges are bulging with students, there is keen competition among the professions for new members. Despite the large increase in college population and the growing urge for professional and graduate study on the part of undergraduates, each of the professional fields fears that it suffers from neglect. Education, engineering, medicine, social service, and the sciences are all recruiting vigorously for students. The enticement of large scholarships, special programs, and other lures for one field or another crowd the college bulletin boards. Every student with academic promise has a wide range of choice, not to mention an assortment of pressures, temptations, and influences, about his career. The top students, of course, are fought over; playing upon their career plans are all the many forces, tangible and intangible, which focus upon top talent, always a scarce item and now under the greatest pressure of demand.

Must we continue to think, along with Justice Frankfurter, that law is largely studied by default rather than by plan? In the keen competition for talent, what hope is there for a profession chosen by default? Do not the earnest efforts of the American Bar Association to impress the public with the nobility of law and the vital role of the lawyer reach the young? Is it really all just a matter of choosing whether to go to work, get drafted, or go to law school?

Whatever the process is, be it choice or default, the law schools and the legal profession are responsible for how the law will fare in this contest for the young. It is hard to face this responsibility because we know so little about the movement of young people into law. We are ignorant even about the simple mechanics of career choices, not to mention the subtleties which play a vital role in causing students to pick one profession in preference to another. In particular, we have little information about how students shift their ambition from one field to another as they proceed through college, though the choices made at this period are obviously critical. The effect of background, the action of attitudes and expectations, and the influence of academic standing must be analyzed before one can properly understand these choices. And such an understanding must be the foundation of any effort intended to increase the inventory of talent for the legal profession.

This study marks the beginning of the search for understanding in this area. It is an objective examination of a group of young people, many wanting to be lawyers since beginning college, others shifting into or out of law as a career, that undertakes to tell us about their origins, background, achievement, limitations, aspirations, and expectations. Much is revealed that is important and useful for all who are concerned with the profession and its future. Indeed, so much is given that the sheer mass of data tends to overwhelm the reader. Much, too, is included that may be hard to relate directly to the process of career choice and the steps which lawyers and legal educators should take in their efforts to build a stronger profession.

From the study there emerges a general picture of the embryonic lawyer, showing him typed by his origins and molded by social and economic factors. Whether this is good or bad and whether changes are desirable are questions beyond the scope of this research. Nor does the study seek to examine the thought processes and motivations of young people as they move to and from the law as a career. These are matters yet to be considered in further studies, hopefully provoked by this one. This is but a first step in the look at lawyers in the making.

Out of the tables and charts and accompanying commentary, one can derive both satisfaction and concern. It is encouraging to learn that the characteristics which predict academic achievement also tend to predict the choice of law as a career. There is comfort in knowing that the law draws well among the top students in a college class and that it appears to get a "fair share" of the academic talent. But does this drawing power derive from the law's scholarly appeal or from its special attractions for the urban men, high in social status, who also happen to overpopulate the upper academic echelons? Of course, academic performance should be a major influence in the choice of law as a career. But why should social status play just as important a role in the making of this choice? Here the study results are discomforting. Equality of opportunity being an important goal of our society, one would have hoped that the law would be a shining example of that equality. But the study shows that in its attractions and appeal to young people the law seems to do its fishing in restricted waters stocked largely with the product of professional families, private schools, and the upper social strata.

The bar and law schools, too, have always taken pride in the belief that anyone with intelligence and industry could become a lawyer. The Lincoln tradition, the study of law at night, the apprenticeship in the law office, are all visions to which lawyers cling in their notion that the doors to a legal career are open to everyone. Yet, the following pages show that reality may call for a different view, even though the study extends only to college graduates and therefore does not provide a complete picture of recruitment to the law. To the credit of the law schools, it does appear that among the college graduates, talent has the greatest influence in determining which students realize their plans to study law. But when academic talent is held constant, social, economic, and religious factors and academic origins play a role which seems incompatible with the belief that equal opportunities exist for all who want to study law.

One question that presents itself immediately is whether the distribution of lawyers to clients will follow the student patterns revealed in this research. If there is such a distribution, the law schools can expect continued disappointment in any efforts to produce lawyers who will want to represent the criminal, the underprivileged, or the family in trouble. Aiding the weak, the oppressed, the poor, and the needy is not the likely end product of a professional system so status oriented in its roots.

What can be done? This is hard to say, for the problems are not only complex but seem to be interrelated in the sense that each factor feeds upon the other. The college students see the profession as it is and then judge other opportunities accordingly. This starts a cycle of inbreeding, a self-selection which makes tomorrow's lawyers like those of yesterday. Trying to break the mold from which new law students are cast, when we cannot change the structure of the profession as it is, will not be easy.

Education and communication are the major weapons for such an effort. The old myths about "overcrowding" and the starving start in practice should be put to rest. Students everywhere should learn about the wide range of opportunities in practice, in public service, and in finance and industry. Here is a job for both the bar and the law schools, and it is one upon which both are already hard at work. The study shows that these efforts have not yielded good results so far. This is not surprising, since years of neglect have allowed the attitudes about the legal profession to crystallize. In this connection it is interesting to note how difficult it is to find out who really influences students as they think about the future. Included in the total study but not reported in the final publication are responses which show that the counsel of neither advisers, teachers, nor parents can be credited with major effect upon the choice of a career. This leads only to the thought that students draw their own conclusions, which makes it the more imperative that students be well informed about the opportunities, the challenges, and the rewards of a lawyer's life.

We all know how difficult it is for young people to appreciate the lawyer's work and his responsibilities. Most students have had virtually no contact with lawyers. Their impressions about the profession derive from television, movies, and fiction. Considering their exposure to other fields and the skilful salesmanship of competing professions, the need is clear to provide information about the law. To reach the student groups which are now neutral or disaffected calls for more than token gestures. There should be a task force at work, armed with facts and figures, whose mission is to reach the young in time for them to learn that a lawyer's life is attainable, not just for the elite, but for all who combine reasonable ability with character and industry and the urge to serve their fellow man.

Anything we do will be an empty effort, however, unless ways can be found to assure qualified students that a legal education is available regardless of financial limitations. Here is another challenge for the law schools and the bar, and it is also one that both are moving forward to meet. In the competition for students, like it or not, money is the major weapon. There are vast scholarship programs for students who wish to become scientists or teachers. In comparison with other career and graduate study fields, the law rates low both in assistance sought and stipends granted. An essential part of the effort to increase the number and quality of law students will be providing means for them to meet the costs of legal education. Without substantial assistance of this sort, the law cannot hold its own against the pressure and temptations exerted upon good students by the other disciplines.

The study shows that the law schools must examine their present scholarship procedures to make sure that their programs are properly geared to talent and need. In some law schools scholarship grants appear to be unrelated to talent, so that weak students have as good a chance for assistance as good ones. In one large group of law schools it seems that a large percentage of students who were both "rich" and "not bright" held scholarship stipends. Can it really be true that there are law schools that equally reward the stupid rich and the bright poor? Here, indeed, there must be a re-examination of policies, since it is simple nonsense to administer financial aid in such a perverse fashion.

The evidence of this study shows that the recent decision of the American Bar Association to support a revolving loan fund for law students is most timely. With this in mind, it is encouraging to note that most law students, including those with large need, have reached the first year of law study with a relatively low debt accumulation. In the preliminary report (not included in the final study) there are indications which show that a "loan for tuition plus living expenses which would not have to be paid back until I was out of law school" would make it possible for many students with law career plans to enter law school who under existing arrangements were postponing entrance because no such help was available.

Another issue illuminated by this study is the problem of law-school dropouts. On the basis of past experience in law schools, it could be expected that about 60 per cent of the students who begin law school will complete the course and receive their degree. This has been a serious problem for legal education. Much time and energy has been devoted to students who have not graduated. Originally, it was hoped that the group under study would include enough of these dropouts to discover any special characteristics that may identify this group. This hope was frustrated, however, by the sheer persistence of the law students in the study group. As the final material was collected, only fifty-three dropouts had been found, too small a sample for sound statistical evaluation. In this connection it must be reiterated that the group under study consists entirely of college graduates. It may be that the traditional heavy dropout in law school consists largely of those who begin their law studies short of this standard. (Also, it may be that the traditional dropout pattern in law schools has changed in recent years.)

For this and other reasons, it would be well to expand these studies to include every type of law student. Despite the excellence and scope of the present work, it does not provide a measure of the characteristics of law students as a whole, nor does it indicate what may be the differences between those with a full college program and the early entrants to law school.

Of great interest to all lawyers who have faced the "slings and arrows of outrageous fortune" are the employment expectations of these young people. Here, too, is an area for exploration in which virtually no previous work has been done. Because this study deals only with first-year law students, it presents no real opportunity to develop a full understanding of the students' employment aspirations. Ordinarily it is not until after the first year in law school that students form their plans. Yet what is revealed here calls for concern. The aspirations of these first-year students indicate their belief that choice legal opportunities depend in a large part upon social and academic credentials. This belief is confirmed in important measure by the recent researches of others, notably Jerome Carlin and Erwin O. Smigel. Does this belief discourage students who are outside "acceptable" social and academic circles from even considering the possibility of law?

Much more could be said about this work. There is regret among its sponsors that it must be incomplete, and that the research is not scheduled to go on. How interesting it would be to follow this group of law students through school and into practice! Much could be learned about legal education, bar examinations, and the often traumatic step from law school into practice. It is sad, too, that the work has been necessarily confined to information obtained only by questionnaire. Insights now lacking could have been revealed if arrangements had permitted actual interviews with students.

In another sense, though, it may be well that no more was undertaken than has been accomplished. As the study stands, it provides a wealth of information which should serve to generate new thought about the legal profession. The present study will serve its purpose if it does no more than this. Now that a start has been made, perhaps there will be further attention given these problems, for it is always easier to work a field once the sod is broken.

LOUIS A. TOEPFER
Vice-Dean
Harvard Law School

1
Recruitment
I. Decisions in College

Where do America's future lawyers come from? How many enter college aspiring to a career in law? How many of those who prefer law at the time of entry to college sustain this interest throughout the four years of undergraduate study? How many change their minds and move on to other fields? Do replacements fill the gaps left by the defectors? In this chapter we will analyze that segment of the college population included in the spring, 1961, survey comprising those who, either as freshmen or as seniors, intended to become lawyers.

The framework for analyzing change and stability in career choice is provided by a classification of students on the basis of their career preference. Since more than 90 per cent of all students selecting law are men, women are excluded from consideration throughout the report. As a result, comparisons are not obscured by sex-related differences. In addition, this chapter excludes students who had no freshman career preference. The resulting classification of male respondents on the basis of their career preference as freshmen and as graduating seniors produced the distribution shown in Table 1.1.

Table 1.1 shows that 916 male students maintained their freshman preference for law, 878 seniors switched into law, and another 674 students abandoned their freshman preference for law and chose other fields. Thus 58 per cent of the freshmen oriented to law still planned legal careers at the time of graduation. Among graduating seniors who selected this career field, 51 per cent chose law early in college and the remainder transferred into law from other fields. Thus the career field of law experienced a modest net gain in potential manpower during the undergraduate years of the June, 1961, class. As we have shown, this gain resulted from heavy traffic in and out of the field.

What accounts for the traffic? Are "early choosers," "late choosers," and "defectors" distinguishable types? And how do the three compare with students who never mentioned law as a potential career?

SOCIAL ORIGINS

Let us locate prospective lawyers in the American social structure. Our data indicate, first, that the component of the June, 1961, graduating class from which law schools recruited their complement of students differed to a marked degree from the remainder of the student population in terms of social background, and second, that the sharpest differences usually occurred when students always expecting to pursue law as a career were contrasted with students never considering this career field.

In comparison with non-lawyers, students endorsing law as a career were significantly higher in social status. Social status is determined by the possession or lack of it of those attributes most highly valued by society's members. Since the determinants of status in American society are education, income, and employment in certain occupational categories, sociologists employ a number of indices to gauge the relative social standing of the individual in the social system. Whether it was the occu-

Table 1.1 Distribution of Men Preferring a Law Career As College Freshmen or As Seniors

Freshman Career Preference	Senior Career Preference		
	Law	Other	Total
Law	916	674	1,590
Other	878		878
Total	1,794	674	2,468

pation of the head of the household, family income, or parental level of education being considered, students who had always preferred law ranked higher than those students who came to law at a later point in time. The social status of the late choosers, in turn, stood above the group of defectors. All three groups, furthermore, ranked above students who never considered a career in law.

Table 1.2 shows that the number of early law aspirants coming from families whose household head was a professional is twice that of non-lawyers (41 per cent for the first group and 20 per cent for the second). Conversely, prospective lawyers were less likely to come from families where the household head was in a manual occupation. The differences are just as strong when family income is considered (Table 1.3); among those selecting law early, 35 per cent reported family incomes in excess of $15,000 as compared with the non-lawyers, of whom 12 per cent came from families in this income bracket. As a group, prospective lawyers came from wealthier families. Since occupation, income, and education are highly correlated, it is hardly surprising that 46 per cent of the students always preferring law indicated that their fathers had a bachelor's degree or had gone on for graduate or professional degrees, while only 21 per cent of the fathers of non-lawyers received a bachelor's degree or a professional or graduate degree (Table 1.4). In addition, mothers of 24 per cent of the former as compared with 16 per cent of the latter completed college or obtained an advanced or professional degree (Table 1.5).

Thus all four measures point to the same conclusion: prospective lawyers tended to be recruited disproportionately from one segment of the population and college graduates anticipating a legal career ranked higher in social standing than other students in the June, 1961, graduating class. Furthermore, inspection of the tables reveals that the group switching into law, in the aggregate, stood between the group always preferring law and the group switching out of law. Stated somewhat differently, the social attributes of students switching into law more closely resembled those who consistently maintained this career preference, while students moving out of law into other fields were

Table 1.2 Parental Occupation and Career Preference

Parental Occupation	Freshman-Senior Career Preference			
	Law Law (Per Cent)	Not Law Law (Per Cent)	Law Not Law (Per Cent)	Not Law* Not Law (Per Cent)
Professional	41	31	28	20
Proprietor or manager	29	32	32	24
Sales (other than sales manager or administrator)	8	8	8	7
Clerical	5	5	6	6
Skilled worker	6	10	11	19
Semiskilled worker	5	4	4	8
Service worker	2	3	5	4
Unskilled worker	2	2	4	4
Farmer or farm worker	2	4	2	8
Total	100	99	100	100
N	879	852	655	1,557

N	3,943
NA on parental occupation	138
Total N	4,081

Note: The first term in the column heads is the freshman preference; the second term is the senior preference.
*This column is based on a representative subsample (1,613) of those males who neither as freshmen nor as seniors expressed a career preference for law.

Table 1.3 Parental Income and Career Preference

Annual Parental Income	Freshman-Senior Career Preference			
	Law Law (Per Cent)	Not Law Law (Per Cent)	Law Not Law (Per Cent)	Not Law* Not Law (Per Cent)
Less than $5,000	8	12	11	20
$5,000–$7,499	16	20	21	29
$7,500–$9,999	16	16	18	18
$10,000–$14,999	17	16	16	13
$15,000–$19,999	11	10	8	4
$20,000 and over	24	21	17	8
Don't know	8	5	8	7
Total	100	100	99	99
N	871	855	655	1,567

N	3,948
NA on parental income	133
Total N	4,081

*See footnote to Table 1.2.

Table 1.4 Father's Education and Career Preference

Father's Highest Educational Attainment	Freshman-Senior Career Preference			
	Law Law (Per Cent)	Not Law Law (Per Cent)	Law Not Law (Per Cent)	Not Law* Not Law (Per Cent)
Eighth grade or less	11	15	18	24
Part high school	9	16	14	18
High-school graduate	19	17	23	22
Part college	15	14	14	15
College graduate	16	18	15	11
Graduate or professional degree beyond the bachelor's	30	21	16	10
Total	100	101	100	100
N	886	860	658	1,575

N	3,979
NA on father's education	102
Total N	4,081

*See footnote to Table 1.2.

Table 1.5 Mother's Education and Career Preference

Mother's Highest Educational Attainment	Freshman-Senior Career Preference			
	Law Law (Per Cent)	Not Law Law (Per Cent)	Law Not Law (Per Cent)	Not Law* Not Law (Per Cent)
Eighth grade or less	7	11	15	18
Part high school	9	14	13	17
High-school graduate	35	31	36	35
Part college	24	20	16	15
College graduate	20	20	15	13
Graduate or professional degree beyond the bachelor's	4	4	5	3
Total	99	100	100	101
N	889	861	656	1,576

N	3,982
NA on mother's education	99
Total N	4,081

*See footnote to Table 1.2.

less like the group loyal to law throughout the four years of college and more like the aggregate of students who never considered this field.

Occupations differ in the social composition of their members in a number of ways. In addition to social status, the religious origins of prospective lawyers should be considered. Table 1.6 shows that 60 per cent of the male non-lawyers were reared as Protestants, but only 41 per cent of the early aspirants to law and 47 per cent of the latecomers to law were reared in the United States' majority religion. Catholics comprised one-quarter of the student group never considering law, but they constituted fully one-third of the graduating seniors preferring this field. Furthermore, they both overchose law as entering freshmen and tended to abandon the field by the time they graduated. Jews were similar to Catholics in their propensity for anticipating a career in law as entering freshmen. Unlike Catholics, Jews also tended to move into law from other career fields by the end of their senior year. The body of young men selecting law at the end of four years of college is overrepresented by members of minority religions.

Table 1.6 Religion in Which Respondent Was Reared and Career Preference

Religion	Freshman-Senior Career Preference			
	Law Law (Per Cent)	Not Law Law (Per Cent)	Law Not Law (Per Cent)	Not Law* Not Law (Per Cent)
Protestant	41	47	45	60
Roman Catholic	36	32	41	25
Jewish	20	18	10	8
Other	1	1	1	3
None	2	2	3	4
Total	100	100	100	100
N	891	851	661	1,576

N	3,979
NA on religion	102
Total N	4,081

*See footnote to Table 1.2.

Correlatively, the career field of law is highly urban—future lawyers are more frequently recruited from metropolitan and other urban areas than are students in general. In examining Table 1.7, we see that three out of ten graduating seniors intending to study law were located in either the central city or the suburbs of a metropolitan area with more than two million population; two out of ten non-lawyers had these demographic characteristics. On the other hand, 52 per cent of the students headed for other careers attended high school in a community numbering less than 100,000 in population, but only 37 per cent of the stable aspirants and 45 per cent of the recruits to law were in this category. Davis found that "students from larger cities more often choose law, but this tendency can be explained by the religious and SES [socio-economic status] composition of those from larger hometowns" (Davis, 1965, p. 152).

We can summarize this section by noting that the socio-religious and urban character of the students aspiring to legal careers is strikingly different from that of students in general. Next, we wish to ask whether differentiation occurs as well in intellectual potential and academic performance.

Table 1.7 Size of Hometown during High School and Career Preference

Size of Hometown during High School	Freshman-Senior Career Preference			
	Law Law (Per Cent)	Not Law Law (Per Cent)	Law Not Law (Per Cent)	Not Law* Not Law (Per Cent)
Metropolitan area				
More than 2,000,000	29	29	23	19
500,000–2,000,000	17	14	18	13
100,000–499,999	17	13	17	15
Less than 100,000	27	32	29	30
Rural	10	12	14	22
Total	100	100	101	99
N	884	860	663	1,582

N	3,989
NA on hometown	92
Total N	4,081

*See footnote to Table 1.2.

ACADEMIC CHARACTERISTICS

A casual perusal of the journals of various professional organizations in the United States reveals that one theme is repeated regularly: there is concern that Profession X is not getting its share of talented students. This is true of the legal profession as well. How did law study fare in the competition for the talent of the June, 1961, graduating class? To answer this and other related questions, a measure of academic performance was constructed on the basis of the student's reported cumulative grade point average, with a correction introduced for the variation among schools in the ability of their students. Using the mean score of a sample of entering 1959 freshmen on the National Merit Scholarship Corporation Qualifying Test, Davis and Bradburn ranked 114 of the 135 schools in the sample (Davis, 1964, pp. 26–31). This ranking was used to adjust the reported grade point average. The result is an Academic Performance Index (API) that divides the students into three groups: the top fifth, above average, and the bottom half. It was found that the following social characteristics predict academic achievement: (*a*) sex—women do better than men; (*b*) socioeconomic status—students from high-status families get better grades than do low-status students; (*c*) religion—Jews do better academically than Gentiles; and (*d*) size of community—students from large cities outdo their counterparts from smaller ones.

With the exception of sex (law is a masculine field), the characteristics that predict academic achievement also predict the choice of law as a career. Table 1.8 shows that the number of graduating seniors preferring law found among the top 20 per cent was twice that of male students in general. Thus law secured more top students than would be allowed by chance because it attracted urban, high-status men who were disproportionately Jewish. Furthermore, the academic quality of law aspirants improved slightly during the four years. This is explained by the fact that although equivalent proportions of the academically talented students moved into and out of law, the net result was an upgrading in the academic caliber of the group preferring law at the time of graduation because more students switched into law (878) than left it (674). While the data do not invite analysis of long-term trends, the field of law clearly attracted a disproportionate number of talented students in the June, 1961, graduating class. We will see that the record of academic achievement will be a crucial variable in assessing what happened to prospective lawyers after their graduation from college.

Just as performance and social status importantly influence the likelihood of the choice of a legal career, so do the academic origins of undergraduates play a role in the selective process. What kinds of undergraduate schools did the four types of students attend? Table 1.9 shows that law aspirants who chose early were more likely to have attended private schools (67 per cent) than male students at large (51 per cent). The schools attended by future lawyers required higher tuition payments, and they were more frequently Class A and Class B schools as measured by the School Quality Index. In sum, a composite portrait of the career field of law includes differentiation in terms of academic origins: prospective lawyers are more likely than other June, 1961, graduates to have completed their college

Table 1.8 Academic Performance Index and Career Preference

API	Freshman-Senior Career Preference			
	Law Law (Per Cent)	Not Law Law (Per Cent)	Law Not Law (Per Cent)	Not Law* Not Law (Per Cent)
Top 20 per cent	30	22	21	17
Above average, but not top 20 per cent	37	38	36	32
Bottom half	33	40	43	51
Total	100	100	100	100
N	907	867	660	1,587

	N	4,021
	NA on API	60
	Total N	4,081

*See footnote to Table 1.2.

careers at private schools that charge high tuition and enroll
students of superior academic caliber.

OCCUPATIONAL VALUES

While connections are found between the career choice of law
and a variety of structural factors that are social and academic in
character, there are other determinants of vocational choice as
well. A growing body of research shows that interests and values influence occupational preferences; indeed, occupational
values and occupational career choices tend to become aligned
through time to achieve consistency. Those filling out the first
questionnaire were asked to indicate which values might be
important to them in selecting a job or a career. Table 1.10

Table 1.9 Characteristics of Undergraduate College and
Career Preference

	Freshman-Senior Career Preference			
College Characteristics	Law Law (Per Cent)	Not Law Law (Per Cent)	Law Not Law (Per Cent)	Not Law* Not Law (Per Cent)
Control				
Private	67	60	61	51
Public	33	40	39	49
Total	100	100	100	100
Tuition				
Less than $900	35	33	23	20
$900 or more	65	67	77	80
Total	100	100	100	100
School quality†				
A (higher)	18	18	14	7
B	9	7	5	7
C	59	59	63	51
D (lower)	14	16	18	35
Total	100	100	100	100
N	916	878	674	1,613
	N = 4,081			

*See footnote to Table 1.2.
†Based on mean scores of sample of entering 1959 freshmen on National Merit Scholarship Corporation Qualifying Test. Used as a gross estimate of average intelligence of student body.

Table 1.10 Occupational Values and Career Preference

Occupational Values[†]	Freshman-Senior Career Preference			
	Law Law (Per Cent)	Not Law Law (Per Cent)	Law Not Law (Per Cent)	Not Law* Not Law (Per Cent)
Making a lot of money	48	55	38	30
Opportunities to be original and creative	40	46	56	52
Opportunities to be helpful to others or useful to society	66	67	58	57
Avoiding a high-pressure job which takes too much out of you	8	8	14	16
Living and working in the world of ideas	39	43	40	38
Freedom from supervision in my work	32	34	25	21
Opportunities for moderate but steady progress rather than the chance of extreme success or failure	16	13	28	34
A chance to exercise leadership	58	63	61	47
Remaining in the city or area in which I grew up	11	10	8	8
Getting away from the city or area in which I grew up	4	10	12	11
Opportunity to work with people rather than things	58	60	54	45
None of these	1	1	1	2
N	915	878	674	1,611

N = 4,078
NA on values = 3
Total N = 4,081

*See footnote to Table 1.2.
†Multiple choices were permitted. Totals therefore equal more than 100 per cent.

shows that the trends in selection from among the eleven items confirm our impression that prospective lawyers are "different" from non-lawyers and that changers more closely resemble their counterparts in the newly selected field than they resemble students in the field they abandoned.

Specifically, future lawyers consider the following values important: making a lot of money; a chance to help others and to be useful to society; freedom from supervision; and an opportunity to work with people. In contrast to non-lawyers, they attach less importance to originality and creativity, avoidance of a high-pressure job, and the need for steady progress rather than a boom-or-bust career. While these are differences in the aggregate, distinctive value profiles would undoubtedly emerge if aspiring lawyers were classified by social origins and anticipated career line as well (see Chap. 7).

Not only were the social origins and occupational values differentiated as the class of 1961 approached graduation, but trends were already discernible that indicated a distinctive mode of occupational integration with the market place. Asked about their most likely employer for full-time work in their anticipated career field, one-half of the prospective lawyers said they were destined for employment in "a private company with fewer than one hundred employees or a professional partnership" or in government office (federal, for the majority). One-third visualized an entrepreneurial career (Table 1.11). The image of law as a traditional profession manned by sturdy, self-reliant sole practitioners apparently commended itself only to a minority of future lawyers. On the other hand, the entrepreneurial life was mentioned by three times as many law aspirants as non-lawyers; among the latter, one in ten circled "self-employed." Defectors from law also mentioned government as a source of employment, but there the resemblance to the ultimate group of law aspirants stopped. Table 1.11 shows that defectors expected to be employed by private companies with one hundred or more employees and in universities, colleges, and school systems.

Of course, expectations for employment reflect much more than personality differences; they also mirror the reality of the world of work. Nevertheless, one would guess that prospective lawyers who value freedom from supervision, show lack of concern for safe, steadily progressing careers, and do not care to avoid high-pressure jobs are destined more for entrepreneurial work settings than are other lawyers.

CAREER CHOICE AND THE LAW SCHOOL ADMISSION TEST PROGRAM

The Law School Admission Test (LSAT), administered by the Educational Testing Service, is a three and one-half hour test required for admission to some eighty accredited law schools which constitute about two-thirds of the fully accredited law schools in the United States. It was "designed to make it pos-

Table 1.11 Anticipated Career Employer and Career Preference

Anticipated Career Employer†	Freshman-Senior Career Preference			
	Law Law (Per Cent)	Not Law Law (Per Cent)	Law Not Law (Per Cent)	Not Law* Not Law (Per Cent)
Private company with 100 or more employees	20	27	35	37
Private company with fewer than 100 employees or professional partnership	48	52	12	11
Family business	8	4	6	3
Self-employed	34	35	9	10
Research organization or institute	1	1	2	7
College or university or junior college	3	4	21	14
Elementary or secondary school or school system	2	0	12	17
Other educational institutions (e.g., technical vocational school)	0	0	0	1
Federal government	26	28	26	16
State or local government	12	10	8	5
Hospital, church, clinic, welfare organization, etc.	0	0	5	6
Other	6	5	4	3
N	914	872	664	1,601

N	4,051
NA on career employer	30
Total N	4,081

*See footnote to Table 1.2.
†Multiple choices were permitted. Totals therefore equal more than 100 per cent.

sible for applicants having the mental abilities necessary for the study of law to make good scores on the test regardless of the undergraduate curricula they had engaged in" (Winterbottom and Johnson, 1961). The Educational Testing Service searched its files for all graduating seniors who were in the NORC sample and who had ever considered a legal career. The aptitude scores of those applicants who had competed the test were made available to NORC for this study.

Table 1.12 shows that 77 per cent of those choosing law early took the LSAT at some time during the two years preceding graduation from college; a slightly lower proportion of the students making the switch into law (71 per cent) was located in the files of the Educational Testing Service. The remaining scores were secured from some 21 per cent of those who had chosen law early and who, at the time of graduation, were seeking careers in other fields; however, they had applied for and completed the LSAT before graduation. The early choosers ranked slightly higher on test taking as compared to the group of graduating seniors transferring into law. This pattern parallels the relation between the two groups in respect to the "lawyer" characteristics presented earlier in the chapter.

The same pattern in rates of test taking is found when the graduating seniors committed to law are classified by selected social and academic characteristics. Just as socio-economic

Table 1.12   Freshman-Senior Career Preference and Law School Admission Test Status

Freshman-Senior Career Preference	LSAT Status		Total (Per Cent)	Base N
	Took LSAT (Per Cent)	Did Not Take LSAT (Per Cent)		
Law/law	77	23	100	916
Not law/law	71	29	100	878
Law/not law	21	79	100	674

N	2,468
Career: never law	1,613
Total N	4,081

status, religious origins, academic performance, and the like predicted the choice of law as a career field, so did they predict the likelihood of applying for and completing the LSAT. Specifically, Table 1.13 shows that rates of test taking were directly related to socio-economic status. Similarly, the urban student, the Jewish student, and the younger student all completed the test more frequently than others when the group is classified by urban-rural origins, religious background, and age.

A similar conclusion may be drawn from inspection of Table 1.14, where rates of test taking are given with reference to certain academic characteristics. It can be seen that students were more likely to complete the test if they ranked high on the API and were graduated from Northeastern and North Central privately controlled schools that charge high tuition fees — schools in Level I (schools highly productive of students who end up with the doctorate) and schools of top quality.[1]

[1]The following tables on LSAT performance are based on the 1,610 men who, in our sample, took the LSAT before college graduation, whether or not they expressed a career preference for law as seniors.

Table 1.13 Background Characteristics and Law School Admission Test Status*

a. Income of Parental Family and LSAT Status

Family Income	LSAT Status		Total (Per Cent)	Base N
	Took LSAT (Per Cent)	Did Not Take LSAT (Per Cent)		
Less than $5,000	62	38	100	172
$5,000 – $7,499	69	31	100	303
$7,500 – $9,999	67	33	100	282
$10,000 – $14,999	77	23	100	289
$15,000 – $19,999	78	22	100	181
$20,000 or more	85	15	100	388

N	1,615
NA on family income	179
Senior career not law	2,287
Total N	4,081

*Among men committed to law as college seniors.

(Table 1.13 continued)

Table 1.13 *Continued*

b. Father's Education and LSAT Status

Father's Highest Education	LSAT Status		Total (Per Cent)	Base N
	Took LSAT (Per Cent)	Did Not Take LSAT (Per Cent)		
Eighth grade or less	55	45	100	225
Part high school	73	27	100	219
High-school graduate	71	29	100	310
Part college	77	23	100	246
College graduate	84	16	100	300
Graduate or professional degree	79	21	100	446

N	1,746
NA on father's education	48
Senior career not law	2,287
Total N	4,081

c. Mother's Education and LSAT Status

Mother's Highest Education	LSAT Status		Total (Per Cent)	Base N
	Took LSAT (Per Cent)	Did Not Take LSAT (Per Cent)		
Eighth grade or less	56	44	100	163
Part high school	67	33	100	199
High-school graduate	75	25	100	579
Part college	75	25	100	384
College graduate	83	17	100	356
Graduate or professional degree	83	17	100	69

N	1,750
NA on mother's education	44
Senior career not law	2,287
Total N	4,081

Finally, rates of test taking can be compared on the basis of the fall, 1961, plans of the group in the sample. Table 1.15 indicates that nine out of ten seniors with definite plans for graduate or professional study immediately after college graduation were located in the files of the Educational Testing Service, with

Table 1.13 *Continued*

d. Size of Hometown during High School and LSAT Status

Size of Hometown	LSAT Status		Total (Per Cent)	Base N
	Took LSAT (Per Cent)	Did Not Take LSAT (Per Cent)		
Metropolitan area				
More than 2,000,000	79	21	100	505
500,000–2,000,000	79	21	100	269
100,000–4999,999	70	30	100	264
Less than 100,000	72	28	100	516
Rural	64	36	100	190

N	1,744
NA on hometown	50
Senior career not law	2,287
Total N	4,081

e. Original Religion and LSAT Status

Original Religion	LSAT Status		Total (Per Cent)	Base N
	Took LSAT (Per Cent)	Did Not Take LSAT (Per Cent)		
Protestant	71	29	100	765
Catholic	76	24	100	594
Jewish	83	17	100	323

N	1,682
Religion "other" and "none"	60
NA on religion	52
Senior career not law	2,287
Total N	4,081

f. Age and LSAT Status

Age	LSAT Status		Total (Per Cent)	Base N
	Took LSAT (Per Cent)	Did Not Take LSAT (Per Cent)		
20 or younger	82	18	100	113
21	79	21	100	886
22	73	27	100	479
23–24	61	39	100	153
25 or older	57	43	100	148

N	1,779
NA on age	15
Senior career not law	2,287
Total N	4,081

LSAT scores on record; among those who were indefinite but planning on further study in the future, only one in four took the aptitude test. Since a great majority of the accredited law schools require the results of the test before they will consider the application for admission, it follows that the test is another barrier the motivated law aspirant must overcome before embarking upon professional training. In effect, the range of findings on test taking suggests that those who did not apply for and complete the LSAT indicated that they were not ready to translate career aspirations into concrete activity.

We have found that the pattern of test completion follows very closely the one discerned for the choice of law as a career field. The next question to be considered is "What are the social and academic correlates of performance on the LSAT?" Table 1.16 shows that the earlier theme is repeated, although with minor variations. The socio-economic correlates of LSAT scores conform to the pattern found in practically all paper-and-pencil tests devised by test-makers, namely that the more

Table 1.14 Academic Characteristics and Law School Admission Test Status*

a. Academic Performance Index and LSAT Status

API	LSAT Status		Total (Per Cent)	Base N
	Took LSAT (Per Cent)	Did Not Take LSAT (Per Cent)		
High	84	16	100	457
Medium	78	22	100	664
Low	64	36	100	653

N	1,774
NA on API	20
Senior career not law	2,287
Total N	4,081

*Among men committed to law as college seniors.

Table 1.14 *Continued*

b. Characteristics of College Attended and LSAT Status

College Characteristics	LSAT Status		Total (Per Cent)	Base N
	Took LSAT (Per Cent)	Did Not Take LSAT (Per Cent)		
Private, tuition $900 or more	86	14	100	609
Private, tuition under $900	75	25	100	533
Public	62	38	100	652
Northeast	81	19	100	800
North Central	78	22	100	507
West	64	36	100	245
South and South Central	55	45	100	242
Level I (high productivity)†	77	23	100	689
Level II	76	24	100	772
Level III	66	34	100	249
Level IV (low productivity)	54	46	100	84
A quality	87	13	100	323
B quality	82	18	100	145
C quality	74	26	100	1,060
D quality	52	48	100	266

N	1,794
Senior career not law	2,287
Total N	4,081

†"School productivity" was measured by the absolute number of students in each college ultimately securing the doctoral degree.

favorably his family is located in the social stratification system, the higher the score of the test subject. Specifically, the mean score of students whose household heads are in white-collar occupations invariably ranked higher than the mean LSAT score of those from blue-collar families (Table 1.16*a*). The mean score of students whose fathers' educations had stopped at the eighth grade or sooner was 489, in contrast to the 530 scored by those whose fathers secured graduate or professional degrees (Table 1.16*b*). The use of the mother's education as the criterion yielded a similar spread (Table 1.16*c*). A comparable variation in performance based on family income, however, shows one

interesting discrepancy: aspiring lawyers from poor families
—those whose incomes were less than $5,000—ranked above
their fellow aspirants whose family incomes ranged from $5,000
to $9,999 (Table 1.16*d*). There is a hint here that young men from
poor circumstances must perform at higher levels to overcome
the handicap of their social origins, because of the heavily over-
weighted social composition of the law career group.

Religious differentials in mean scores on the LSAT are similar
to those found on API among the graduating seniors planning on
careers in law (Table 1.16*e*). In both instances Catholics rank
lowest. Only 14 per cent were high on API, in contrast to the
27 per cent of the Protestants and the 35 per cent of the Jews
who scored high. The mean score on the LSAT for Catholics
was 504; for Jews, 517; and for Protestants, 523—the highest
mean score of the three major religious faiths.

Urban origins also correlate with performance on this test.
Students who were reared in metropolitan areas with a population of two million or more scored highest (a mean of 525); in
contrast, legal aspirants from urban areas with fewer than 100,000
population or from rural areas ranked lowest, in the aggregate, with a mean score of 508 (Table 1.16*f*). These differences

Table 1.15 Plans for Graduate or Professional Study and Law
School Admission Test Status*

Plans Index	LSAT Status		Total (Per Cent)	Base N
	Took LSAT (Per Cent)	Did Not Take LSAT (Per Cent)		
Definitely going, fall, 1961	88	12	100	1,050
Tentatively going, fall, 1961	75	25	100	264
Definitely going, future	41	59	100	360

N	1,674
Other plans	32
NA on plans	88
Senior career not law	2,287
Total N	4,081

*Among men committed to law as college seniors.

Table 1.16 Background Characteristics and Law School Admission Test Score*

a. Parent's Occupation and LSAT Score

Parent's Occupation	LSAT Score		Base N
	Mean	Standard Deviation	
Professional	525	95	574
Proprietor/manager	519	87	514
Sales	507	82	148
Clerical	530	95	58
Skilled worker	486	98	105
Semiskilled worker	484	71	54
Service worker	462	74	46
Unskilled worker	489	74	33
Farmer or farm worker	508	74	22

N	1,554
NA on parent's occupation	56
Total N	1,610

b. Father's Education and LSAT Score

Father's Highest Education	LSAT Score		Base N
	Mean	Standard Deviation	
Eighth grade or less	487	74	169
Part high school	501	84	191
High-school graduate	508	90	271
Part college	513	95	235
College graduate	528	89	301
Graduate or professional degree	531	94	405

N	1,572
NA on father's education	38
Total N	1,610

*Among all men who took the LSAT.

(Table 1.16 continued)

Table 1.16 *Continued*

c. Mother's Education and LSAT Score

Mother's Highest Education	LSAT Score		Base N
	Mean	Standard Deviation	
Eighth grade or less	492	88	128
Part high school	493	83	178
High-school graduate	513	87	515
Part college	515	93	325
College graduate	533	93	359
Graduate or professional degree	538	85	71

N	1,576
NA on mother's education	34
Total N	1,610

d. Income of Parental Family and LSAT Score

Family Income	LSAT Score		Base N
	Mean	Standard Deviation	
Less than $5,000	517	91	132
$5,000–$7,499	496	92	263
$7,500–$9,999	499	85	231
$10,000–$14,999	521	93	274
$15,000–$19,999	534	81	164
$20,000 or more	530	89	387

N	1,451
NA on family income	159
Total N	1,610

e. Original Religion and LSAT Score

Original Religion	LSAT Score		Base N
	Mean	Standard Deviation	
Protestant	523	91	651
Catholic	504	87	570
Jewish	517	94	312

N	1,533
Religion "other" and "none"	43
NA on religion	34
Total N	1,610

Table 1.16 *Continued*

f. Size of Hometown during High School and LSAT Score

Size of Hometown	LSAT Score		Base N
	Mean	Standard Deviation	
Metropolitan area			
More than 2,000,000	525	88	458
500,000–2,000,000	524	92	262
100,000–499,999	515	91	239
Less than 100,000	508	91	447
Rural	498	86	163

N	1,569
NA on hometown	41
Total N	1,610

may be due to the socio-economic and religious differentials in population composition that characterize different degrees of urbanization.

Some institutional characteristics of the colleges and universities of arts and sciences graduating students for whom LSAT scores are available were used to classify performance of students on this aptitude test. The results obtained are shown in Table 1.17. Students graduating from "productive" schools (Level I) had a mean score of 541 while the Level IV students scored an average of 433. The spread of some 108 points in mean scores testifies to the qualitative differences in American institutions of higher learning. Other institutional characteristics that differentiate performance on the LSAT can be described as follows: Region—graduates of colleges in the Northeast scored highest while those from southern and South Central schools were at the bottom. Tuition and control—graduates of private colleges and those charging high tuition fees did better than students from other schools.

Performance on the LSAT correlates with the Plans Index as well. The mean score for students who definitely planned to go on to graduate or professional study in fall, 1961, was 528, while the score dropped to 504 for students with definite plans for

Table 1.17 Characteristics of College Attended and Law School Admission Test Score*

College Characteristics	LSAT Score		Base N
	Mean	Standard Deviation	
Level I	541	88	625
Level II	508	91	697
Level III	484	76	240
Level IV	433	75	48
Northeast	531	89	769
West	523	85	183
North Central	502	86	486
South and South Central	472	97	172
Private	522	90	1,113
Public	499	89	497
Tuition $900 or more	547	86	613
Tuition under $900†	495	88	997
	N = 1,610		

*Among all men who took the LSAT.
†Includes all public institutions.

Table 1.18 Plans for Graduate or Professional Study and Law School Admission Test Score*

Plans Index	LSAT Score		Base N
	Mean	Standard Deviation	
Definitely going, fall, 1961	528	86	1,073
Tentatively going, fall, 1961	477	87	225
Definitely going, future	504	97	210

N	1,508
Other plans	22
NA on plans	80
Total N	1,610

*Among all men who took the LSAT.

going in the future (Table 1.18). Perhaps the most striking finding was the relatively low level of performance of those tentatively slated for professional or graduate study in fall, 1961; these 225 subjects averaged only 477 on this aptitude test.

Members of the legal profession have been concerned that perhaps the academic potential of students defecting from law or initially choosing other career fields is superior to that of graduates who do elect law. Although rates of test taking were especially low among the defectors, the mean scores of those who did complete the test are revealing. The defectors from law show the lowest mean score (a mean of 493); those recruited to the field during college scored substantially higher (a mean of 527), even outranking the aspirants who maintained their freshman orientation to this career (a mean of 510). In sum, the data presented in Table 1.19 support the earlier conclusion that the changes of career fields during the four years of college result in a net improvement in the academic quality of future lawyers.

A final topic that deserves consideration in reporting on the LSAT and the career choice of law is relationship between the LSAT and the two components of the Academic Performance

Table 1.19 Freshman-Senior Career Preference and Law School Admission Test Score*

Freshman-Senior Career Preference	LSAT Score		Base N
	Mean	Standard Deviation	
Not law/law	527	92	625
Law/law	510	86	703
Law/not law	493	101	140
N	1,468		
Other career	142		
Total N	1,610		

*Among all men who took the LSAT.

Index employed in the NORC researches. Since both purport to measure academic achievement, it follows, as Davis (1965, pp. 246–48) has noted, that

When LSAT scores are tabulated simultaneously by GPA [grade point average] and the School Quality Index, [these] relationships should obtain: (*1*) Within a school quality level, mean LSAT scores should increase with increasing GPA. (*2*) Within a GPA level, mean LSAT scores should increase with school quality.

Within a school quality group, the higher the GPA, the higher the LSAT. Because the LSAT has a standard deviation of 100, we can say that in A-level schools there is a range in means of .73 sigma units from the A– GPA group to the C level; in C schools, the range is 1.1 standard deviation.

Within a GPA level, the higher the school quality, the higher the mean LSAT. For cells with sufficient cases, the range from A to D school quality within a GPA group is in the neighborhood of 1 standard deviation.

It is interesting to note that C+ students in the A schools have means about the same as B+ and A students in C- and D-level schools, and C or worse students in A-level schools surpass B students in levels B, C, and D. . . . The two components of API do correlate with [LSAT].

Table 1.20 Mean Law School Admission Test—Weighted N*

School Quality	GPA					
	≧ A–	B+	B	B–	C+	≦ C
I	621 (26)	612 (41)	588 (75)	585 (90)	574 (59)	548 ↑(37)
II	[579 (21)]		528 (31)	543 (38)	506 (33)	– (9)
III	576 (47)	551 (105)	515 (168)	491 (245)	477 (239)	465 (143)
IV	[↓574 (21)]		490 (30)	445 (55)	430 (48)	433 (34)

Note: Both components of API are associated with LSAT scores.
*Davis, 1965, Table A–3.1 (p. 247).

2

Recruitment
II. Entry into
Law School

In the preceding chapter attention was given to the correlates of career choice among the June, 1961, graduating classes. The choice of law as a career was shown to be linked with a variety of social characteristics, all suggesting that by the time a young man has received his baccalaureate at one of America's colleges of arts and science, substantial selection — social, academic, and personal — has been completed. The chances for embarking upon a legal career are clearly *not* randomly distributed. However, the word and the deed are not one and the same. How many men who indicated a career preference for law actually entered a law school during the academic year following graduation? In this chapter we examine the recruitment and entry into law school of some of those graduating seniors who named law as their long-run career choice and assess some factors that account for initiation of legal study.

ENTRY INTO LAW SCHOOL

In the spring of 1962 NORC mailed follow-up questionnaires to the entire sample of 35,000 students, including the prospective lawyers. Over 94 per cent of the aspiring lawyers had returned their completed questionnaires by the time field work was completed. These 1,697 students comprised the cohort whose law-school status was being investigated one year after graduation.

It was learned that some 69 per cent of all graduating seniors who had elected a career in law reported in the following year that their current (or most recent) field of study was law. We will show later that the process by which two out of every three aspirants began their legal studies was strongly related to the social and academic origins of the graduates. First, it will be helpful to say something about the problem of entry into law school in relation to the fall, 1961, career plans of the graduating seniors.

Given the relatively favorable socio-economic circumstances of law aspirants, it is not surprising that many of these students reported definite plans for graduate and professional study.[1] In the spring of 1961, about eight out of ten prospective lawyers said they planned to attend graduate or professional school in the fall of 1961, and two out of three already had been accepted by one or more schools. In contrast to this extensive planning for graduate and professional study, less than one-half of the former law aspirants and just over one-third of all male students questioned planned to begin graduate study in the fall of 1961 (Table 2.1).

Why should there be such differences? The most important reason appears to be that students slated for other fields planned to begin by obtaining employment in their fields. But while education or engineering majors, for example, can expect to find work in their field of interest without further training, students going on in law or medicine after their undergraduate work are barred from their future profession without further study.

The result, as shown in Table 2.2, is that those seniors oriented to law who had definite fall plans were virtually all enrolled for study in a law school at the time of their graduation. Nine out of ten reported law as their field of study in the one-year follow-up; one out of twenty was enrolled in graduate school in other fields of study; and only one out of twenty had been deflected from "definite" plans for enrollment. Among those "tentatively" slated for graduate or professional study, about two out of three were in law school. Another one out of six were graduate students, while the proportion not enrolled at

[1]Advanced work, the reader is cautioned, does not necessarily mean immediate entry into law school.

Table 2.1 Plans for Graduate or Professional Study and Career Preference

Plans Index	Freshman-Senior Career Preference			
	Law Law (Per Cent)	Not Law Law (Per Cent)	Law Not Law (Per Cent)	Not Law* Not Law (Per Cent)
Definitely going, fall, 1961	66	57	31	24
Tentatively going, fall, 1961	16	16	13	12
Definitely going, future	18	24	32	30
Tentatively going, future	0	2	8	13
Not going	0	1	16	22
Total	100	100	100	101
N	870	836	629	1,546

N	3,881
NA on plans	200
Total N	4,081

*See footnote to Table 1.2.

Table 2.2 Plans for Graduate or Professional Study and Fall, 1961, Activity*

Plans Index	Fall, 1961, Activity			Total (Per Cent)	Base N
	Law School (Per Cent)	Graduate School (Per Cent)	Not Attending (Per Cent)		
Definitely, fall, 1961	91	5	4	100	977
Tentatively, fall, 1961	64	15	21	100	242
Future	9	9	82	100	351

N	1,570
Other plans	82
NA on plans	45
NA on activity	97
Total N	1,794

*Among men committed to law as college seniors.

all increased to about one out of four. Finally, of those who said they would enroll in graduate or professional study in the future, more than eight out of ten were not enrolled for any study in 1961–62. One out of ten of the remainder was in law school or in graduate school. For the most part, students did what they set out to do.

However, the plans of college seniors were vulnerable to change in differing degrees. Table 2.3 shows that definite plans

Table 2.3 Academic Performance Index, Plans for Graduate or Professional Study, and Fall, 1961, Activity*

Plans and Activity (Fall, 1961)	Academic Performance Index		
	High (Per Cent)	Medium (Per Cent)	Low (Per Cent)
Definitely, fall, 1961			
Law school	91	91	91
Graduate school	5	5	3
Not attending	3	4	6
Total	99	100	100
N	331	389	248
Tentatively, fall, 1961			
Law school	–	70	56
Graduate school	–	13	16
Not attending	–	17	28
Total	–	100	100
N	18†	84	135
Future			
Law school	3	18	9
Graduate school	12	5	5
Not attending	85	77	85
Total	100	100	99
N	60	109	182

N	1,556
NA on API	14
Other plans	82
NA on plans	45
NA on activity	97
Total N	1,794

*Among men committed to law as college seniors.
†Too few cases to compute.

were virtually impervious to change regardless of undergraduate performance as measured by the API. Whether the students were in the top twenty, in the bottom half, or in between, nine out of ten entered one kind of law school or another. Among those tentatively committed to graduate or professional study, on the other hand, API did make a difference. There were almost no high API students who were uncertain of their fall plans in the spring of 1961, but of the uncertain ones, the above average student was more likely to begin legal study than the student in the bottom half. In the group initially disposed to "future" study, the high API student was far less likely to be in law school than his counterparts of lesser academic ability and more likely to be enrolled in graduate study. The initial decision to defer study and the last-minute turnabout may have denied him access to the law school of his choice, hence the greater likelihood that he would go into graduate work.

A similar pattern emerges when another correlate of the career choice of law — religious origins — is considered (Table 2.4). In the "definite" category, no differences obtained among the three religious groups, although there were Jew-Gentile differences among those tentatively going in the fall of 1961. Jews are most likely to be in law school, least likely to be in graduate study, and least likely as well not to be enrolled at all. Among the students planning on future study, there were no religious differences in entry to law school, but Jews again were more likely to embark upon graduate study than were their Protestant and Catholic counterparts.

A consideration of the combined factors of family income and fall plans yields further evidence that the crystallization of plans by the spring of 1961 leads directly into some form of legal study. Among those definitely planning to attend law school, 88 per cent of the students from families with 1961 incomes of less than $7,500 were in law school, a percentage only slightly smaller than that observed among the more affluent (Table 2.5). Among those with only tentative plans, family incomes of $15,000 or more provided a significant advantage in beginning the first year of law but no advantage in entering a graduate school. Of the men with future plans for graduate or professional study, students of families with top incomes simply did not bother to go, in contrast with the others whose rate of entry to both law school and graduate school was higher.

Correlatively, another measure of social status—the father's occupation—indicates that blue-collar and farm families yield students with definite plans who are slightly less likely to go to law school than their counterparts who are more favorably located in the occupational structure; however, if their plans are

Table 2.4 Original Religion, Plans for Graduate or Professional Study, and Fall, 1961, Activity*

Plans and Activity (Fall, 1961)	Original Religion		
	Protestant (Per Cent)	Catholic (Per Cent)	Jewish (Per Cent)
Definitely, fall, 1961			
Law school	91	92	92
Graduate school	4	3	6
Not attending	5	5	3
Total	100	100	101
N	403	292	240
Tentatively, fall, 1961			
Law school	61	64	82
Graduate school	21	13	9
Not attending	19	23	9
Total	101	100	100
N	97	87	34
Future			
Law school	12	11	14
Graduate school	3	4	14
Not attending	85	85	73
Total	100	100	101
N	163	136	22

N	1,474
Religion given as other and none	53
NA on religion	43
Other plans	82
NA on plans	45
NA on activity	97
Total N	1,794

*Among men committed to law as college seniors.

tentative, they are much less likely to enter law school but more likely to enter graduate study. They are relatively most likely of any group to enter law school if their spring, 1961, intention was to go "in the future" (Table 2.6).

As we shall see later, academic origins play a pivotal role in the distribution of law students within the American system of legal education. Because of this it is instructive to examine fall

Table 2.5   Income of Parental Family, Plans for Graduate or Professional Study, and Fall, 1961, Activity*

Plans and Activity (Fall, 1961)	Income of Parental Family		
	Less Than $7,500 (Per Cent)	$7,500– $14,999 (Per Cent)	$15,000 or More (Per Cent)
Definitely, fall, 1961			
Law school	88	92	92
Graduate school	4	5	4
Not attending	8	3	4
Total	100	100	100
N	219	302	429
Tentatively, fall, 1961			
Law school	59	57	70
Graduate school	13	15	15
Not attending	28	28	15
Total	100	100	100
N	61	81	87
Future			
Law school	11	18	7
Graduate school	8	7	2
Not attending	82	75	91
Total	101	100	100
N	141	108	87

N	1,515
NA on family income	55
Other plans	82
NA on plans	45
NA on activity	97
Total N	1,794

*Among men committed to law as college seniors.

Lawyers in the Making

plans in relation to the NORC measure of undergraduate school quality (Table 2.7). Again, among the "definites," quality of school attended has no bearing on rates of entry. It is among the tentatively committed that undergraduate school quality is important; only 5 per cent of those from A schools were out of residence during the year following graduation, as compared with 38 per cent among the products of D schools. In addition,

Table 2.6 Parental Occupation, Plans for Graduate or Professional Study, and Fall, 1961, Activity*

Plans and Activity (Fall, 1961)	Parent's Occupation			
	Professional (Per Cent)	Proprietor, Manager (Per Cent)	Sales, Clerical (Per Cent)	Blue Collar, Farm (Per Cent)
Definitely, fall, 1961				
Law school	91	94	91	86
Graduate school	5	4	3	6
Not attending	4	3	5	8
Total	100	101	99	100
N	364	308	117	153
Tentatively, fall, 1961				
Law school	77	57	70	48
Graduate school	11	16	4	23
Not attending	12	27	26	29
Total	100	100	100	100
N	73	70	27	61
Future				
Law school	10	8	6	17
Graduate school	5	4	11	6
Not attending	85	88	83	76
Total	100	100	100	99
N	81	91	47	126

N	1,518
NA on parent's occupation	52
Other plans	82
NA on plans	45
NA on activity	97
Total N	1,794

*Among men committed to law as college seniors.

some 80 per cent of the A school graduates planning only tentatively to attend in the fall did then enroll in law school, while only 30 per cent of the D school graduates acted similarly. In fact, there were more students from the latter stratum in graduate school than in law school, the only reversal in magnitude that we have found so far. The proportions in graduate school from the remaining types of colleges range from 9 per cent from

Table 2.7 Quality of Undergraduate College, Plans for Graduate or Professional Study, and Fall, 1961, Activity*

Plans and Activity (Fall, 1961)	Undergraduate School Quality†			
	A (Per Cent)	B (Per Cent)	C (Per Cent)	D (Per Cent)
Definitely, fall, 1961				
Law school	91	93	90	96
Graduate school	6	4	4	3
Not attending	3	3	6	1
Total	100	100	100	100
N	232	83	563	98
Tentatively, fall, 1961				
Law school	80	62	68	30
Graduate school	15	19	9	32
Not attending	5	19	23	38
Total	100	100	100	100
N	20	21	161	37
Future				
Law school	—	19	12	10
Graduate school	5	11	5	10
Not attending	95	70	83	80
Total	100	100	100	100
N	42	27	193	93

N	1,570
NA on plans	45
Other plans	82
NA on activity	97
Total N	1,794

*Among men committed to law as college seniors.
†See footnote to Table 1.9.

C colleges to 19 per cent from B colleges. Among those planning to attend "in the future," it is striking that nobody who graduated from an A-quality college attended graduate school and only 5 per cent entered law school, while from two to four times as many from other colleges enrolled in law school and from 5 to 11 per cent were taking graduate courses. People from A schools have an accurate forecast of their plans, it would appear.

The question of academic performance aside, the fact of attending an A rather than a D-quality school is clearly an important factor in determining the shape and character of the future careers of the June, 1961, graduates. In sum, our analysis shows that fall plans are highly determinative of entry into graduate or professional school but undergraduate academic performance, religious origins, and socio-economic status play predictable roles in selecting enrollees from among those who only tentatively planned to go on for graduate or professional study.

Fall plans aside, how did academic records (API), religious origins, and social status affect the probability of legal study during the first year following graduation?

ACADEMIC PERFORMANCE AND RELIGIOUS ORIGINS

In Table 2.8 rates of entry are presented, with religious origins and API examined simultaneously. Within each religious

Table 2.8 Original Religion, Academic Performance Index, and Law-School Attendance* (Per Cent Attending Law School, Fall, 1961)

Original Religion	Academic Performance Index			Total
	High	Medium	Low	
Jewish	87 (107)	80 (122)	74 (77)	81 (306)
Catholic	76 (78)	66 (205)	58 (262)	63 (545)
Protestant	73 (198)	71 (276)	47 (250)	63 (724)

N	1,575
Religion given as other and none	59
NA on religion	46
NA on API	17
NA on fall, 1961, activity	97
Total N	1,794

*Among men committed to law as college seniors.

category, students with low API as undergraduates showed lower rates of entry than did others, and Jews surpassed Protestants and Catholics in rates of entry to law school in each of the three categories of academic performance. Furthermore, Jews who scored low on API were as likely to enter law school as were Protestants of superior academic standing, perhaps testifying to the propensity for law among Jews even when their undergraduate record would appear to make the study of law a hazardous undertaking.

Protestants who were in the middle API range enrolled more frequently than Catholics of similar API, but Catholics from the bottom half of the academic heap went on more frequently than did their Protestant counterparts. Finally, a comparison of Jews and Gentiles shows that the margin in percentage differences between the two steadily increases as one descends the ladder of talent. All in all, a complicated relationship emerges that is clarified to some degree by the measuring of the quality of the law schools that these students attended.

ACADEMIC PERFORMANCE AND FAMILY INCOME

An examination of the joint effects of family income and API in Table 2.9 reveals that both factors work together to influence the probability of entry into law school. The bright students who came from families with 1961 incomes of $15,000 or more went to law school twice as frequently as the low API students whose family incomes were $7,500 or less. Among the high API students, family income played a negligible role in determining rates of entry, but at the middle and low levels of academic performance, chances of entry definitely improved with each successive increment in income. Only 40 per cent of the "poor," low API men in contrast with 65 per cent of the "wealthy," low API men made it to law school. Significantly, talent exerts a greater influence on entry to law school than does family income; however, talent diminishes in influence the greater the family income of the law aspirant. It is especially important for the "poor" young man to perform well in college if he is to undertake the study of law.

We find very much the same results if father's occupation or father's education is employed to gauge socio-economic status.

Thus law school claimed less than one-half of the low API college seniors from families whose household heads were in blue-collar occupations, in contrast to 82 per cent of the high API students reared in families of professional men (Table 2.10). Similarly, the low API student whose father completed less than eight years of school had only one chance in two of beginning the study of law as compared with 86 per cent of the high API seniors whose fathers had taken graduate or professional degrees (Table 2.11).

API AND FRESHMAN CAREER FIELD

The analysis has shown that academic achievement as measured by the API was an important variable in selecting the graduating seniors who were likely to be in law school during the year immediately following graduation. Its importance in selecting prospective lawyers, however, was tempered by other socio-religious factors. It remains to be seen whether timing of career choice affected rates of entry as well. In the preceding chapter, "early" and "late choosers" of the career field of law

Table 2.9 Income of Parental Family, Academic Performance Index, and Law-School Attendance* (Per Cent Attending Law School, Fall, 1961)

Income of Parental Family	Academic Performance Index			Total	
	High	Medium	Low		
$20,000 or more	77 (125)	83 (157)	80 (91)	80 (373)	
$15,000–$19,999	78 (51)	70 (67)	51 (59)	66 (177)	
$10,000–$14,999	76 (70)	73 (93)	68 (107)	72 (270)	
$7,500–$9,999	80 (50)	66 (107)	49 (104)	62 (261)	
$5,000–$7,499	73 (45)	55 (99)	50 (139)	55 (283)	
Less than $5,000	70 (33)	65 (72)	25 (64)	51 (169)	

N	1,533
NA on parental income	147
NA on API	17
NA on fall, 1961, activity	97
Total N	1,794

*Among men committed to law as college seniors.

Table 2.10 Parental Occupation, Academic Performance Index, and Law-School Attendance* (Per Cent Attending Law School, Fall, 1961)

Parental Occupation	Academic Performance Index			Total
	High	Medium	Low	
Professional	82 (177)	71 (219)	62 (165)	72 (561)
Proprietor, manager	74 (128)	73 (193)	57 (178)	68 (499)
Sales, clerical	66 (47)	65 (82)	64 (76)	65 (205)
Blue-collar, farm	64 (47)	67 (126)	38 (185)	52 (358)

N	1,623
NA on father's occupation	57
NA on API	17
NA on fall, 1961, activity	97
Total N	1,794

*Among men committed to law as college seniors.

Table 2.11 Father's Education, Academic Performance Index, and Law-School Attendance* (Per Cent Attending Law School, Fall, 1961)

Father's Highest Education	Academic Performance Index			Total
	High	Medium	Low	
Graduate or professional degree	86 (146)	85 (145)	73 (105)	82 (396)
College graduate	72 (72)	62 (113)	48 (103)	59 (288)
Part college	73 (37)	63 (106)	63 (100)	65 (243)
High-school graduate	74 (80)	62 (90)	50 (105)	61 (275)
Part high school	64 (39)	68 (84)	44 (108)	52 (231)
Eighth grade or less	62 (37)	76 (88)	49 (101)	62 (226)

N	1,659
NA on father's education	21
NA on API	17
NA on fall, 1961, activity	97
Total N	1,794

*Among men committed to law as college seniors.

were compared with each other, with freshmen who abandoned their career choice of law at some time before graduation, and with those male graduating seniors who had never been interested in law. The findings consistently supported the proposition that latecomers to the career field of law resembled the early deciding law aspirant while the "defectors," in the aggregate, were less "lawyer-like" in their social, academic, and personal characteristics. How, then, do early and late choosers compare on rates of entry to law school? What are the outcomes when freshman career fields are specified?

Some 71 per cent of the early aspirants and 64 per cent of those who switched to law from another freshman career field reported one year later that law was their current or most recent field of study. This difference of 7 per cent in rates of entry is consistent with other findings that demonstrate that those who chose law early were slightly higher than the latecomers on aggregate measures of the personal, social, and academic characteristics that predict a preference for this career field. This is true even though the two types of law aspirant converged in terms of social origins, career plans, and the like, when compared with students preferring other career fields.

Table 2.12 Freshman Career Field, Academic Performance Index, and Law-School Attendance* (Per Cent Attending Law School, Fall, 1961)

Freshman Career Field	Academic Performance Index			Total	
	High	Medium	Low		
Law	81 (231)	75 (267)	58 (242)	71 (740)
Medicine	96 (27)	76 (49)	62 (47)	75 (123)
English	72 (40)	61 (92)	50 (78)	60 (210)
Other professions	60 (25)	60 (40)	53 (47)	58 (112)
Business	57 (23)	62 (50)	46 (70)	53 (143)
Social sciences	— (5)	76 (24)	—	59 (46)
Physical sciences	— (17)	— (16)	62 (17)	54 (59)
Biological sciences	— (−)	— (1)	— (26)	— (1)
Education	— (8)	— (14)	— (1)	49 (35)
Humanities	— (5)	— (1)	— (13)	— (14)
				— (8)

*Among men committed to law as college seniors.

Table 2.12 shows the freshman career field preferences of latecomers to law in relation to the API. With the exception of one field (business), the API makes a difference in rates of entry for every freshman career field sending students into law. Furthermore, with the exception of the freshman career choice of medicine, an early choice of law invariably resulted in higher rates of entry into law school than did other fields at comparable levels of undergraduate academic performance. Following medicine and law, freshman career fields supplied entering law students from their high API groups in the following descending order: English, other professions, and business. Among medium API students, the order is social science, business, English, etc. Fully 96 per cent of the high API students abandoning medicine for law and 81 per cent of the early law choosers went to law school, while only a minority (46 per cent) of the low API students switching from business into law did so.

3

The Role
of Occupational
Inheritance

The preceding chapters have indicated that socio-economic status, religion, and academic performance in college are all associated with choice of law as a career. Our purpose in this chapter is to examine these same attributes in the light of a significant item of information not originally available at the time the first questionnaire in this study was administered — whether or not the student has a lawyer parent. This datum was gathered in the first-year follow-up to the original study and was subsequently subjected to extensive analysis (Zelan, 1964).

The analysis is based only on the 33,492 male cases in the NORC study. Women have been excluded because they comprise a proportionately negligible part of the legal profession.[1] Our presentation will involve the relationships between a series of social background variables and four dependent variables representing at least three stages of occupational choice behavior in college. These stages, referred to earlier, are original choice of law, retention in law, and recruitment to law. The end product of their interaction we call senior choice of law. They are defined in the note to Table 3.1.[2]

THIS CHAPTER WAS CONTRIBUTED BY JOSEPH ZELAN.

---

[1]Fewer than 5 per cent of the respondents who indicated a preference for a legal career were women. The proportion of female members of the bar in 1961 was less than 3 per cent (American Bar Foundation, 1961).

[2]Respondents were instructed to choose from a list of 108 occupational

One would expect to find that parental occupation plays a significant role in a student's career choice. In an earlier study of father's and son's occupations (Rogoff, 1950), 23 per cent of the lawyers in the sample had lawyer fathers, higher than any other occupation. The effect on choice of law of having a lawyer parent is correspondingly impressive among the students in the present survey (Table 3.1).[3] Among lawyers' sons, 29 per cent report an original preference for law as contrasted with only 4 per cent of sons of non-lawyers. Through a process of greater retention and recruitment of lawyers' sons, this difference increases by the senior year to 35 versus 5 per cent. Although introduction of variables other than parental occupation serves to increase further our predictive ability, none is as pronounced in its effect as the single characteristic of having a lawyer parent.

Our next task is to determine whether the relationship previously considered between socio-economic status and choice of law is no more than a reflection of the effect of having a lawyer parent, or whether socio-economic status continues to be pre-

---

specialties in indicating their "career preference when [they] started college," their "anticipated career field," and "any alternative career field seriously considered during college." Retrospective data about past decisions obviously have shortcomings which could be avoided by doing a panel study beginning with college freshmen. On the one hand, the recollections of the respondents are subject to distortion. On the other hand, we have no data for those students who failed to reach the senior year of college. The present data provide no way out of the first hazard, and we have no way of determining its incidence. The second factor is probably not serious as it pertains to choice of law, for it turns out that those attributes associated with choice of law are some of the same attributes associated with finishing college. If the college dropouts were included in our tabulations, they would probably serve merely to strengthen the associations we have found.

[3]There is a difference between the case base shown in Table 3.1 and the previously mentioned 33,492 male cases because the data on lawyer parents were not gathered until the second wave of the study, one year after the initial questionnaire distribution. Attrition during this phase of the study resulted in reduction of the number of cases available for analysis.

The question on parental occupation required the respondent to indicate if either of his parents had ever been a lawyer. No separate tabulation is available for fathers and mothers, though the sex composition of the legal profession makes it unlikely that many mothers are here included.

Lawyers in the Making

dictive of choosing law even among the sons of non-lawyers. Table 3.2 shows the relationship between socio-economic status and choice of law among sons of non-lawyers.[4] Since lawyer parents are by definition all high in status, no comparable table for sons of lawyers is necessary. This table tells us that the original relationship between high status and law as a career choice was almost entirely due to the lawyer fathers in the high-status category. The small differences between high and low socio-economic status are statistically significant at the .05

[4]The index of socio-economic status is composed of father's occupation, father's education, and income of parental family. It is identical to that used by Davis (1964, pp. 17–21).

Table 3.1 Choice of Law by Parental Occupation

Parental Occupation	Per Cent Choosing Law*			
	Original	Retention	Recruitment	Senior
Lawyer	29 (789)	84 (230)	15 (559)	35 (789)
Non-lawyer	4 (25,811)	50 (1,079)	3 (24,732)	5 (25,811)

*Original = the percentage of all men who indicated a preference for law at some time prior to the senior year of college.

Retention = the percentage of men indicating an original preference for law who also indicated a preference for law during the senior year.

Recruitment = the percentage of men not indicating an original preference for law who do prefer law during the senior year.

Senior = the percentage of all men who indicated a preference for law at the time the questionnaire was administered.

Table 3.2 Choice of Law by Socio-Economic Status among Sons of Non-Lawyers*

Choice of Law	Socio-Economic Status		Statistical Significance
	High	Low	
Original	6	2	.05
Senior	7	4	N.S.
N	713	805	

*This table is based on a representative subsample of 2,026 men rather than on the total weighted sample. Previous analyses of the NORC data using the representative subsample have found it to approximate very closely the distributions in the total weighted sample.

level only for original choice of law, not for senior choice.[5] Since the differences are negligible as compared with the effect of parental occupation, we can disregard socio-economic status in our subsequent analysis.

Since the analysis in earlier chapters involved a somewhat different format of presentation than the one employed here, we present in Table 3.3 the relationships between choice of law and both the API and religion in terms of the four dependent variables under investigation. We see that those students with high levels of academic performance are more likely to choose law than those of lesser ability.[6] Jews are more likely to choose law than Catholics, and Catholics are more likely to choose law than Protestants. These patterns of occupational choice are true of original choices, retention of original choosers, recruitment among those with a different original choice, and hence among seniors just prior to graduation.

Since both the API and religion are associated with having a lawyer parent, we proceed next to an examination of choice of

[5]The test of significance used here is that appearing in Davies (1962). Since this latter test is intended for simple random samples and our data come from a clustered sample, the percentage differences were adjusted by a factor of 1.5, as recommended by Jacob J. Feldman of NORC.

[6]Our "high" and "low" categories represent a division of the entire study sample into two approximately equal parts. Since women, who are excluded from the present analysis, tend to have somewhat higher API scores, our "high" category contains somewhat less than 50 per cent of the men.

Table 3.3 Choice of Law by Academic Performance Index and Religion

API and Religion	Per Cent Choosing Law			
	Original	Retention	Recruitment	Senior
API				
High	6 (16,459)	59 (1,022)	4 (15,437)	8 (16,459)
Low	4 (16,486)	46 (660)	3 (15,826)	5 (16,486)
Religion				
Jewish	9 (2,816)	71 (244)	7 (2,572)	13 (2,816)
Catholic	7 (8,838)	52 (614)	4 (8,224)	8 (8,838)
Protestant	4 (19,055)	50 (735)	3 (18,320)	5 (19,055)

law by parental occupation and the API (Table 3.4) and choice of law by parental occupation and religion (Table 3.5). Again, each attribute continues to exert an independent effect on choice of law at each of the stages of decision, except for a reversal in the retention rates of Catholics and Protestants. However, since the senior choice pattern depends not only on the rates of choice in the previous three stages, but upon the sizes of the groups to which these rates apply, the impressive 90 per cent retention rate among Protestant sons of lawyers, when applied to the 78 cases in this cell, is insufficient to change the relative rates of choice by religion in the senior year. The rate of senior choice continues to be highest among Jews and lowest among Protestants, with Catholics occupying an intermediate position. Simi-

Table 3.4 Choice of Law by Parental Occupation and Academic Performance Index

Parental Occupation	API	
	High (Per Cent)	Low (Per Cent)
	Original	
Lawyer	31 (534)	25 (246)
Non-lawyer	5 (13,074)	3 (12,331)
	Retention	
Lawyer	85 (164)	79 (62)
Non-lawyer	54 (652)	45 (411)
	Recruitment	
Lawyer	17 (370)	11 (184)
Non-lawyer	4 (12,422)	3 (11,920)
	Senior	
Lawyer	38 (534)	28 (246)
Non-lawyer	6 (13,074)	4 (12,331)

larly, students who are high on the API continue to choose law more frequently than those low on the API. Parental occupation continues to be the major differentiating attribute in choice of law.

Having examined the contributions of parental occupation, academic performance, and religion to the choice of a legal career, we are now in a position to examine these attributes simultaneously. If their independent effects continue to be manifested, we might reasonably expect them to produce a contingency table in which the lowest rate of choice appears in the cell Protestant, low API, and non-lawyer parent, and the highest rate in the cell Jewish, high API, and lawyer parent.

Table 3.5 Choice of Law by Parental Occupation and Religion

Parental Occupation	Religion		
	Jewish (Per Cent)	Catholic (Per Cent)	Protestant (Per Cent)
	Original		
Lawyer	32 (166)	33 (254)	24 (329)
Non-lawyer	7 (2,074)	5 (6,574)	3 (15,134)
	Retention		
Lawyer	87 (53)	68 (85)	90 (79)
Non-lawyer	70 (136)	47 (360)	45 (517)
	Recruitment		
Lawyer	19 (113)	17 (169)	11 (250)
Non-lawyer	7 (1,938)	4 (6,214)	3 (14,617)
	Senior		
Lawyer	41 (166)	37 (254)	30 (329)
Non-lawyer	11 (2,074)	7 (6,574)	4 (15,134)

The actual outcome, however, presents a departure from this expectation. The highest rate of choice of law in Table 3.6 is among Jewish sons of lawyers with low academic performance. Although being Jewish and having a lawyer parent produces a high probability of opting for a legal career, it is the student who performs less well in college who is more likely to make this choice. The dominant pattern of choice whereby the better student chooses law continues to manifest itself among other religions and among all sons of non-lawyers.[7]

[7]Our use of the "high-low" categories of academic performance raises the possibility that students in the same half of the API dichotomy are not in fact similarly distributed. We therefore have attempted to restrict our inferences to comparisons between high and low performers who are otherwise identical on discrete attributes. In any case, our purpose here is to isolate rather gross tendencies which are observable in the consistent patterns of relationships in a table (Kendall and Lazarsfeld, 1950, p. 138).

Table 3.6 Choice of Law by Parental Occupation, Academic Performance Index, and Religion

Parental Occupation	API	Religion		
		Jewish (Per Cent)	Catholic (Per Cent)	Protestant (Per Cent)
		Original		
Lawyer	High	30 (129)	35 (140)	28 (235)
	Low	38 (37)	32 (112)	10 (88)
Non-lawyer	High	8 (1,315)	6 (3,035)	5 (7,613)
	Low	4 (733)	5 (3,461)	3 (7,255)
		Senior*		
Lawyer	High	38	43	35
	Low	51	30	14
Non-lawyer	High	13	7	5
	Low	8	6	3

*N's are identical with those presented under "Original."

An extensive analysis of the "religious factor" in occupational choice by Greeley, utilizing data from this same NORC study, indicated that law and medicine are overchosen by Jews as compared with Protestants and Catholics, and that this difference is especially prominent among students of high-status origins (Greeley, 1963, pp. 53 and 64). If we look only at sons of lawyers and inspect the distribution of choices among law, medicine, and other occupations by academic performance, we note a further refinement of the relationship observed by Greeley (Table 3.7). Among high API students, Jews and Catholics choose law *or* medicine at about equal rates, though Catholics choose law more than Jews and Jews choose medicine more than Catholics. Medicine is the senior year career expectation for as many as 5 per cent of the Jewish sons of lawyers who are in the bottom half of the national graduating class (whether this expectation is realistic is irrelevant here). In the present context, this is impressive evidence for the often mentioned favor shown to medical careers among Jews. The really striking preference of Jews for law and medicine appears among the low API students in Table 3.7. Here we see that only 44 per cent of the Jews choose "other" occupations, whereas 79 per cent of the Catholics and 85 per cent of the Protestants make such choices.

Table 3.7 Senior Career Choice (Law, Medicine, or Other) among Sons of Lawyers, by API and Religion

API	Religion	Career Choice			Total (Per Cent)	Base N
		Law (Per Cent)	Medicine (Per Cent)	Other (Per Cent)		
High	Jewish	38	18	44	100	129
	Catholic	43	12	45	100	137
	Protestant	35	12	53	100	230
Low	Jewish	51	5	44	100	37
	Catholic	21	0	79	100	111
	Protestant	14	1	85	100	84

Recourse to the literature on ethnic and religious differences in mobility aspiration provides one easy explanation for this differential choice of law and medicine by religion. This literature documents the fact that Jews tend to evince a level of aspiration and a pattern of actual social mobility which is among the highest of groups studied (Strodtbeck, 1958). Unfortunately, this explanation becomes somewhat weak here when we remember that the population represented in Table 3.7 consists of young men about to graduate from college whose fathers are lawyers. There may indeed be some differences in the valuation of upward social mobility among members of even so homogeneous a group, but this can hardly serve as the major explanatory mechanism for the differences we have found.

Although the strength of mobility aspirations among students with different religious origins may vary only slightly, it is possible that the observed differences result from a differential subcultural emphasis on the areas in which that mobility is to be sought. We know from previous research that Jews tend to prefer self-employment (Fauman, 1958; Goldberg and Sharp, 1958). In the past, this orientation could and did find expression in small business enterprises. In our day the image (though perhaps not the reality) of self-employment is found principally among the so-called free professions, of which law and medicine are the exemplars. Thus the patterns of occupational choice observed above can in part be explained by a model in which each individual strives to attain an occupational status equal to or higher than that of his father, but with Jews tending to restrict their choices to law and medicine. Since the physician enjoys a higher status position in American society than does the lawyer,[8] the Jewish sons of lawyers who demonstrate higher academic ability will opt for medicine while those of lesser academic ability (and hence relatively disadvantaged in the

[8]In the 1960 Census, lawyers and judges ranked third in annual income among forty-eight "professional, technical and kindred" occupations, surpassed only by physicians and surgeons, and by dentists (U.S. Department of Commerce, U.S. Bureau of the Census, 1963, Table 25). The well-known 1947 NORC study of occupational prestige ranked the lawyer eighteenth among ninety occupations in "general standing." A 1963 replication of that study ranks the lawyer eleventh among the ninety occupations (Hodge *et al.*, 1964, p. 290).

competition for the more rewarding slots) will tend to choose law. Non-Jews who are similarly disadvantaged by lower academic performance will, by this model, perceive a greater range of alternatives from which to choose.

The study from which these data are drawn did not provide an opportunity for the respondents to express a preference for medicine other than by stating it to be an actual or possible alternative career choice. Some sort of abstract expression of preference, as distinct from personal career plans, would be necessary to test the above propositions.[9] However, there was an item which made possible an indirect test. In expressing attitudes about occupations, the students had the opportunity to endorse the statement, "I don't have the ability to do this kind of work." We proceeded on the assumption, based on the work of Festinger, that among persons for whom this statement was equally true the frequency of endorsement would be higher among those for whom medicine was a more attractive choice to begin with.[10] We would thus expect the highest rate of endorsement among low API sons of lawyers to be manifested by the Jews. Table 3.8 indicates that this is indeed so. The explanatory model suggested above is therefore at least consistent with the available data on a subgroup of the June, 1961, college graduating class in American colleges and universities.

[9]Among a series of questions about attitudes toward specific occupations was included the possible response, "My parents would disapprove of my going into this field." Needless to say, hardly any group is characterized by high responses on this item as it pertains to the physician.

[10]"If two elements are dissonant with one another, the magnitude of the dissonance will be a function of the importance of the elements" (Festinger, 1957, p. 16).

Table 3.8 Percentage Saying "I Don't Have the Ability for Medicine" among Low API Sons of Lawyers, by Religion

Religion	"No Ability"	Base N
Jewish	73	37
Catholic	61	112
Protestant	58	88

SUMMARY

An analysis of the role of occupational inheritance in the decision to pursue a career in the legal profession yielded the following conclusions:

1. Having a lawyer parent is the single strongest predictor of choice of law among a series of background characteristics.

2. Socio-economic status has little predictive value independently of parental occupation.

3. Students with higher academic performance are more likely to choose law than those with lower academic performance, even when parental occupation is controlled.

4. Religious origins are predictive of choice of law, with the order of probability being Jewish, Catholic, and Protestant, even when parental occupation is controlled.

5. When parental occupation, API, and religion are considered simultaneously, Jewish sons of lawyers who are low on the API are more likely to choose law than those who are high on the API. The latter group shows a greater choice of medicine than the former. This pattern of choice is explained by recourse to a model in which the mobility aspirations of Jews are more frequently restricted to the free professions than are those of non-Jews.

4

Allocation to American Law Schools

Professions vary in the amount of formal preparation demanded of the neophyte practitioner. The graduate of American colleges of arts and science may assume the title of "engineer" or "teacher" upon receipt of the baccalaureate. The physician or lawyer, however, is required to undertake additional years of professional preparation before the occupational title is legitimately his. To understand the career sequence involving professions in the latter category means knowing what it takes to enter the professional schools and what it takes to succeed in the professional world.

This chapter describes some outcomes of the process by which students hoping to enter the legal profession are distributed among American law schools. Recent research indicates that the division of legal labor in the metropolis is related to the social and academic origins of the lawyers. The large law firm seeks out graduates of elite colleges and elite law schools, men who are talented and preferably Protestant. Information is lacking, however, on the determinants of allocation of college graduates among law schools. Given the structural variety of law schools in the United States, a critical question would be to ask what effects achievement and ascribed social status have on the allocation of prospective lawyers within the multi-tiered system of American legal education. Data on this topic that are

national in scope would make it possible to determine the mode
of integration between the institutional system of legal education
and the organization of the legal profession. It is now possible to
provide some data that contribute to this kind of assessment.

CLASSIFYING LAW SCHOOLS

An analysis of allocation requires a classification of law
schools and an identification of the students who enter various
types of law schools. An inventory of structural characteristics
differentiating law schools might include size of student body,
public or private status, the ratio of nighttime to daytime students, the number of students per full-time faculty, and the like.
Underlying these organizational characteristics is the dimension
of institutional quality; some law schools are considered elite
institutions while others are run of the mill.

In this research, law-school quality is measured by a single
index: the law-school median score of entering students on the
Law School Admission Test (LSAT) administered by the Educational Testing Service.

Of the students who entered law school, 77 per cent completed

Table 4.1 Distribution of First-Year Law Students by
Law-School Stratum*

Law-School Stratum	Per Cent of Students	Number of Students
I	26	284
II	30	335
III	44	484
Total	100	1,103
No information on LSAT		76
Not in law school		421
NA on fall, 1961, activity		97
Total N		1,697

*This and succeeding tables are based on college seniors who
indicated a career preference for law. Those seniors who indicated
some other career preference but who nevertheless entered law
school are excluded from the tabulations.

the LSAT during their junior or senior undergraduate year. With these data, the schools were ranked in three strata.

Stratum I. Eight schools ranking highest on median entering scores. They are usually included in the layman's catalogue of top national law schools. The median entering LSAT score in each school was 572 or higher.

Stratum II. Sixteen schools rank below the top eight on median LSAT scores. The scores range between 485 and 571. While most of these schools would be regarded as solid, substantial schools, they would not rank as top national schools.

Stratum III. The remaining one hundred schools attended by aspiring lawyers in our sample.

The sample of students was distributed among the three types of law schools[1] as shown in Table 4.1. With the classification given in this table, it is now possible to analyze the effects of achievement and ascribed social status on the allocation of entering students to law schools of varying quality.

In Tables 4.2 and 4.3, the distribution of entering students among the law schools is presented in terms of their undergraduate performance and family income. Table 4.2 shows that academic achievement is a prime determinant of placement in law school. Fully 58 per cent of all high API law students entered the top eight law schools; only 3 per cent of the low API students are entwined with ivy or its equivalent. There is a secondary effect, however, when consideration is given to social status as indicated by family income (Table 4.3). Controlling for

[1]Ranking the quality of law schools which these students were attending during the academic year 1961–62 on the basis of such input measures as the LSAT score is open to criticism. But the classification employed in this research correlates highly with rankings on institutional quality of graduate schools of arts and science that were prepared by Berelson (1960). For example, six of the eight law schools in Stratum I are located at universities that also have top quality graduate schools; and ten of the sixteen law schools in Stratum II are at universities with middle-ranking graduate schools. Furthermore, Norman Miller's forthcoming analysis of academic origins and destinations of all June, 1961, bachelor's recipients entering graduate or professional school during the year following graduation from college yields findings on law students that confirm the pattern reported in this monograph.

Table 4.2 Academic Performance Index and Law-School Stratum

API	Law-School Stratum			Total (Per Cent)	Base N
	I (Per Cent)	II (Per Cent)	III (Per Cent)		
High	58	24	28	100	301
Medium	21	38	41	100	451
Low	3	24	73	100	334

N	1,086
NA on stratum	76
NA on API	17
Not in law school	421
NA on fall, 1961, activity	97
Total N	1,697

Table 4.3 Academic Performance Index, Income of Parental Family, and Law-School Stratum

API	Family Income	Law-School Stratum			Total (Per Cent)	Base N
		I (Per Cent)	II (Per Cent)	III (Per Cent)		
High	$7,500 or more	61	23	16	100	229
	Less than $7,500	43	25	32	100	56
Medium	$7,500 or more	23	41	36	100	316
	Less than $7,500	16	34	50	100	101
Low	$7,500 or more	4	23	73	100	228
	Less than $7,500	1	27	72	100	85

N	1,015
NA on stratum	76
NA on API/family income	88
Not in law school	421
NA on fall, 1961, activity	97
Total N	1,697

level of academic achievement, ascription does make a difference. Thus 61 per cent of the bright, "rich" boys entered the top eight schools in contrast with 43 per cent of the bright, "poor" boys. On the other hand, the poor but talented prospective lawyer was twice as likely to be admitted to a Stratum I law school as was the well-to-do but mediocre student (only 23 per cent of the latter did so). The primary effects of talent and secondary effects of social status obtained across the board, with the exception of low API men entering Stratum III law schools where equivalent proportions of each family income group were preparing for the law. Essentially the same pattern appears in Table 4.4, which analyzes achievement and another commonly employed indicator of social status, father's education, and shows their impact on allocation.

Thus a major finding emerges: While the data provide no guidance in specifying the mechanism at work, the end product of the allocative process is that primary emphasis is on the achievement component and ascribed status appears to influence

Table 4.4 Academic Performance Index, Father's Education, and Law-School Stratum

API	Father's Education	Law-School Stratum			Total (Per Cent)	Base N
		I (Per Cent)	II (Per Cent)	III (Per Cent)		
High	Graduate or professional	69	20	11	100	125
	College graduate	49	27	24	100	79
	High school or less	49	28	23	100	107
Medium	Graduate or professional	23	39	38	100	123
	College graduate	27	42	31	100	137
	High school or less	15	37	48	100	180
Low	Graduate or professional	3	23	74	100	77
	College graduate	4	25	71	100	112
	High school or less	2	25	73	100	146

N	1,086
NA on stratum	76
NA on API/father's education	17
Not in law school	421
NA on fall, 1961, activity	97
Total N	1,697

entry to top quality schools only when talent is held constant. The mechanism of self-selection and the mechanism of institutional filtration are probably both at work; the C+ student from Podunk is unlikely to apply to the top eight and when he does, the gatekeepers are unlikely to admit him.

Socio-economic status as indicated by family income and father's education does not exhaust the range of statuses subsumed by the concept of ascription. Another major dimension is the student's religious origin. It is clear that religion is an important determinant of the type of practice the young lawyer is likely to undertake after passing the bar examination. Does religion also influence allocation in American law schools? Table 4.5 considers the joint effects of talent (API) and religious origins. Inspection of the table confirms the importance of talent as a predictor variable but indicates that the pattern of Catholic recruitment to law school differs substantially from Protestant and Jewish patterns, the latter two showing identical distribu-

Table 4.5 Academic Performance Index, Original Religion, and Law-School Stratum

API	Original Religion	Law-School Stratum			Total (Per Cent)	Base N
		I (Per Cent)	II (Per Cent)	III (Per Cent)		
High	Jewish	67	20	13	100	93
	Protestant	61	22	17	100	144
	Catholic	31	35	34	100	59
Medium	Jewish	22	33	45	100	97
	Protestant	20	38	42	100	195
	Catholic	21	45	34	100	135
Low	Jewish	1	11	88	100	57
	Protestant	3	16	81	100	118
	Catholic	3	36	61	100	152

N	1,050
NA on stratum	76
NA on API/religion	53
Not in law school	421
NA on fall, 1961, activity	97
Total N	1,697

tions. Talented (i.e., high API) Catholics were one-half as likely as non-Catholics to be in Stratum I schools and twice as likely to be attending Stratum III schools. Talented Catholics, furthermore, were distributed in equal proportions among the three layers, while two out of three talented Protestants and Jews studied law at the top eight schools. Among Stratum I schools, religious differentials completely disappeared among students of middling or low academic attainment, the divergence between Catholics and non-Catholics reappearing among Strata II and III schools. Stratum II includes many of the prominent Catholic law schools; these schools recruited disproportionate numbers of Catholic law students from the ranks of the mediocre and the bottom half of the June, 1961, graduating classes.

Table 4.6 shows the chances of entry to the top eight schools when students are classified by three attributes: API, parents' religion, and metropolitan origins. Students whose hometown during high school was in the central city or suburb of a metropolitan area with a total population of 500,000 or more were classified as "metropolitan" in origin. Among students entering law school during the year following graduation from college, close to one-half (48 per cent) of the metropolitan Jews entered

Table 4.6 Academic Performance Index, Original Religion, and Metropolitan Origins (Per Cent in Stratum I Law Schools)

API	Original Religion					
	Jewish		Catholic		Protestant	
	Metropolitan	Other	Metropolitan	Other	Metropolitan	Other
High	77 (22)	63 (71)	21 (28)	36 (33)	55 (83)	71 (59)
Medium	41 (32)	12 (65)	17 (64)	25 (68)	22 (129)	17 (66)
Low	— (11)	0 (46)	0 (80)	6 (72)	1 (80)	11 (28)

N	1,037
NA on stratum	76
NA on API/metropolitan	66
Not in law school	421
NA on fall, 1961, activity	97
Total N	1,697

Stratum I schools in contrast to one-tenth of the metropolitan Catholics. It is noteworthy that metropolitan origins had different implications for Jews and Gentiles: among the former, metropolitan origins increased the chances of entry to the top eight; among the latter, the opposite was true.

Further inspection of the table reveals that academic performance carried greater weight in determining allocation in the system than did metropolitan background. Thus Jewish students who were high on the API but not of metropolitan background entered Stratum I schools more frequently than did Jewish students of metropolitan origins scoring only in the middle on API. And some 77 per cent of the metropolitan Jews who scored high on the API entered these schools. Among the Protestants, the greater importance of API is shown by comparing rates of entry to the top eight among high API and medium API students of both types. Furthermore, metropolitan origins made no difference at all if students scored at the middle on API. While the effects of API were slightest among the Catholics, nevertheless they were consistent with the differences noted in the other religious categories.

That patterns of recruitment and selection were determined long before college graduation is suggested by Table 4.7, in which the quality of the undergraduate college is considered together with the student's LSAT score and religious origins. Catholics from A-quality undergraduate colleges of arts and science, many of which share the same campus with Stratum I law schools, were almost as likely to be attending elite law schools as were Protestants and Jews. But relatively few Catholic graduating seniors who intended to become lawyers attended top-quality undergraduate colleges. The table shows that undergraduate origins are even more important than talent in distributing students among law schools. About half of the students attending law schools in Stratum I scored at least 600 on the LSAT but students from elite undergraduate colleges were somewhat more likely to be in these top eight law schools even if they scored below 600 than were students from other undergraduate colleges who scored above 600. It is clear, then, that Catholic representation in elite law schools was handicapped by decisions made four years earlier.

In fact, Table 4.7 suggests that the order of importance of factors determining entry into the top eight is (*1*) the "right" undergraduate school; (*2*) high performance on the LSAT; and (*3*) religious origins. Unfortunately, it is impossible to unravel the ascription-achievement complex beyond this point insofar as it concerns religious origins. Evidently competition for undergraduate slots in the elite colleges makes it difficult for the young man of proper lineage to gain admission to the preferred colleges unless he can compete in the academic market with his non-Brahmin peers.

Table 4.8 supports this interpretation, for it confirms once again the order of importance of undergraduate origins, performance as measured by LSAT score, and family income. At the one extreme, 81 per cent of the students who have attended elite colleges, who score above 600 on the LSAT, and who are born to families with 1961 incomes above $15,000 make their way to Stratum I law schools, in contrast to the 10 per cent of the students who lack all three attributes.

Whatever the reason may be for not attending the "proper" college of arts and science, clearly the consequences four years later are important to the careers of aspiring young lawyers.

Table 4.7 Religious Origins, Law-School Admission Test Score, and Undergraduate School Quality (Per Cent in Stratum I Law School)

Undergraduate School Quality†	LSAT Score	Original Religion		
		Jewish	Protestant	Catholic
A	600 or more Less than 600	82 (33) 60 (30)	80 (49) 43 (54)	75 (12) 40 (10)
B, C, D	600 or more Less than 600	52 (21) 15 (130)	42 (50) 18 (238)	35 (40) 7 (244)

N	911
NA on stratum	76
NA on LSAT score/religion	192
Not in law school	421
NA on fall, 1961, activity	97
Total N	1,697

†See footnote to Table 1.9.

Since the problem of allocation to undergraduate school was beyond the scope of the NORC panel study of career choice (Davis, 1964, 1965), the meaning of attendance at an A-quality college is itself problematical. Does it signify achievement or ascription or both? Performance in high school importantly affects admission to college, particularly to an elite college, but the well-documented socio-economic differentials in rates of entry to college cannot be overlooked. Thus access to professional and technical occupations, including law, is beyond the grasp of a disproportionate number of lower-status youth. Furthermore, while dropping out from college hinges primarily upon academic performance, career choice for those who complete their undergraduate work—and change in career choice during the college years—has a decidedly socio-cultural flavor.

This research, and the work of Davis (1964, 1965), show that those in the June, 1961, graduating classes who as freshmen chose law as a career field ranked significantly higher in socio-economic status than did other career aspirants. In addition, graduating seniors who shifted into law from other career fields

Table 4.8 Law School Admission Test Score, Undergraduate School Quality, and Income of Parental Family (Per Cent in Eight Top National Law Schools—Stratum I)

Undergraduate School Quality†	LSAT Score					
	Score 600 or More			Score 599 or Less		
	Family Income			Family Income		
	$15,000 or More	$7,500– $14,999	Less Than $7,500	$15,000 or More	$7,500– $14,999	Less Than $7,500
A	81 (62)	78 (23)	70 (10)	54 (59)	42 (19)	36 (11)
B, C, D	51 (39)	35 (35)	35 (34)	20 (210)	9 (227)	10 (153)

N	882
NA on stratum	76
NA on LSAT score or family income	221
Not in law school	421
NA on fall, 1961, activity	97
Total N	1,697

†See footnote to Table 1.9.

outnumbered college men who abandoned their freshman choice of law for other fields. Since the newly recruited law aspirants tended to resemble those who maintained their freshman choice of law, the exchange resulted in a group of prospective lawyers even more socially homogeneous than it was four years earlier.

It becomes clear that allocation to law schools functions in two stages. The short-run requisite of choice allocation is academic performance. But decisive social factors that facilitated admission to the professional schools which emphasize performance were at play long before the law school admissions officer examined student dossiers.

From his study of the Detroit bar, Ladinsky (1963) concluded that "family and school background give rise to career contingencies, i.e., they act as social 'filters' impinging upon law practice by differentially screening candidates."

Carlin's work on the New York City bar (1962*a*) also points to the importance of type of college attended, social class, and religious origins in distributing students among law schools. In contrast to the findings here that Jews and Protestants of equivalent talent show identical probabilities of placement in Stratum I schools, Carlin found that Jewish origins place a handicap on entrance to Ivy League law schools, reflecting, perhaps, an admissions policy based on regional quotas that in effect discriminates against New York City Jews. Contradictory findings stem in part from differences in definition and research design. Top national law schools, as defined in the present work, include schools in the Midwest and Far West as well. Also, studies of the metropolitan bar necessarily include lawyers who entered a law school without the baccalaureate, while the NORC survey of career choice is limited to 1961 bachelor's recipients. Despite these differences, all these studies of the legal profession support the proposition that the allocation of future lawyers is in full motion by the time they enter law school.

It is not at all clear that the process runs a smooth, unruffled course; indeed, one could infer that corporate and individual strain often result. Consider, for example, the role of religion. We learn from Smigel (1962, 1964) that the graduating law student who combines lineage, talent, and personality can write his own ticket in the metropolitan job market (see also Lortie,

1958; Carlin, 1962*b*). But only 50 per cent of the talented (high API) entering law students are Protestant. Furthermore, the entering students who are Protestant, graduates of elite colleges, and the offspring of families with 1961 incomes of $15,000 or more comprise a mere 16 per cent of the group of first-year students in Stratum I law schools. Hence, the recruiter for the large law firm may be hard pressed to find the "right" man.

In the face of these constraints, there appear to be two levels of adaptation. In the long run, the overriding need to ensure organizational survival by hiring technically competent professionals may induce firms to widen the sluice gates, recruit the requisite legal talent, and let the social trappings go by the board. Smigel's study of Wall Street firms (1964) indicates that this does occasionally happen. At the same time, student conceptions concerning their future in the law are no doubt influenced by the social barriers to professional recruitment.

Our data suggest that the organization of professional practice does bear on the molding of these preferences. Assuming that law students are not unaware of the predilections of their future profession, it follows that Protestants in Stratum I law schools would have reported preferences for professional partnership more frequently than would their non-Protestant classmates.

And they did. In the one-year follow-up questionnaire, students were asked to report on employment preferences. Among Protestants in Stratum I law schools, 87 per cent mentioned professional partnerships as long-run future employment; among Catholics in these schools, the percentage is 69; among Jews, 67. While the great majority of all students in the elite law schools mentioned professional partnerships (the phrase does not distinguish between the two-man firm and the large metropolitan firm), the religious differential in expectations for this type of life-time employment nevertheless suggests that law students of minority religious origins were already beginning to select themselves out of this kind of legal organization.

The outcome of the recruitment and selection process yields an entering law class in the top law schools that is disproportionately filled with students whose socio-academic characteristics would, in their freshman college year, have predicted a career choice of law.

5

The First
Year of Legal
Study

It is now appropriate to analyze the composition of the students in the three strata of law schools and the different kinds of educational experiences they encounter.

LAW-SCHOOL STRATUM AND SOCIAL COMPOSITION

The outcome of the recruitment and selection process yields an entering law class in the top eight law schools that is disproportionately filled with students whose socio-academic characteristics would in their freshman college year have predicted a career choice of law. Table 5.1 shows that the educational levels of parents, family incomes, and occupational standing of the household head—in short, the key indicators of socio-economic status in American society—become progressively diluted as one descends the institutional ladder. The religious composition, furthermore, is just as unbalanced; Protestants comprise one-half of Stratum I, Jews one-third, and Catholics trail behind, providing only one-fifth of the students. In Stratum II Catholics and Protestants are evenly divided, with the Jewish representation declining by almost one-half, while in Stratum III the mix changes again, with Protestants comprising over two-fifths, Catholics one-third, and Jews about one-fifth. The distinctive combination of each stratum represents the end product of a combination of self- and institutional selection.

The most striking differences are in terms of talent as indicated by undergraduate API. Stratum I, as shown in Table 5.2, is "loaded"; fully 64 per cent of the first-year law students in this

65

Table 5.1 Social Composition of Law-School Strata*

a. Father's Education

Father's Highest Education	Law-School Stratum		
	I (Per Cent)	II (Per Cent)	III (Per Cent)
Graduate or professional degree	42	28	25
College graduate	15	21	12
Part college	14	11	17
High-school graduate	15	12	18
Part high school	6	16	12
Eighth grade or less	8	12	16
Total	100	100	100
N	280	335	482

N	1,097
NA on father's education	6
NA on stratum	76
	1,179
[Not in law school	421][†]
[NA on fall, 1961, activity	97][†]
[Total N	1,697][†]

b. Income of Parental Family

Family Income	Law-School Stratum		
	I (Per Cent)	II (Per Cent)	III (Per Cent)
$20,000 or more	42	31	21
$15,000–$19,999	16	8	11
$10,000–$14,999	15	20	21
$7,500–$9,999	11	17	18
$5,000–$7,499	8	14	21
Less than $5,000	8	10	8
Total	100	100	100
N	262	311	449

N	1,022
NA on family income	81
NA on stratum	76
Total N	1,179

*Men committed to law as college seniors and entering law school.
†These items are the same for all subsequent tables and will henceforth be omitted.

Table 5.1 *Continued*

c. Parental Occupation

Parental Occupation	Law-School Stratum		
	I (Per Cent)	II (Per Cent)	III (Per Cent)
Professional	47	38	33
Proprietor, manager	36	30	32
Sales, clerical	8	13	14
Blue collar, farm	9	20	21
Total	100	101	100
N	273	323	466

N	1,062
NA on parental occupation	41
NA on stratum	76
Total N	1,179

d. Religion

Original Religion	Law-School Stratum		
	I (Per Cent)	II (Per Cent)	III (Per Cent)
Protestant	50	40	43
Jewish	32	18	23
Catholic	19	43	34
Total	101	101	100
N	266	323	470

N	1,059.
Religion given as other and none	25
NA on religion	19
NA on stratum	76
Total N	1,179

stratum were in the high API group in contrast with 12 per cent of the Stratum III students. Consider, furthermore, the academic origins of the students destined for these professional schools: of the men in the June, 1961, graduating classes, some 8 per cent were in A-quality colleges of arts and science; of those in that class seeking a law career, 18 per cent stem from A schools; and of those in Stratum I law schools, fully 51 per cent came from these elite colleges! In contrast, 69 per cent of Stratum III is comprised of students from C-quality schools and another 20 per cent from D-quality schools. Clearly, the stage was set four years earlier when bright and not-so-bright entering freshmen landed on Campus Q rather than on Campus R.

STRATUM AND FALL PLANS

The role of the interrelated personal and institutional mechanisms in the allocation of law-school students is seen more clearly when we examine the firmness of plans for fall, 1961, among those who enrolled as law students in 1961–62. National schools accept applications for admission relatively early in the academic year; as a result fully 95 per cent of those who entered these law schools had been "definite" in their fall plans in spring, 1961, and none at that time had planned on "future" graduate or professional school. In contrast, 72 per cent of those beginning their legal studies in Stratum III schools during the year following graduation had been "definite" in the previous spring; another 21 per cent had been only tentatively going as of spring, 1961; and 7 per cent went despite their spring intentions to defer graduate or professional study.

Table 5.2 Academic Composition of Law-School Strata*

a. Academic Performance Index

Academic Performance Index	Law-School Stratum		
	I (Per Cent)	II (Per Cent)	III (Per Cent)
High	64	23	12
Medium	33	52	37
Low	3	25	51
Total	100	100	100
N	283	330	481

N	1,094
NA on API	9
NA on stratum	76
Total N	1,179

*Men committed to law as college seniors.

Table 5.2 *Continued*

b. Quality of Undergraduate College

Undergraduate College Quality	Law-School Stratum		
	I (Per Cent)	II (Per Cent)	III (Per Cent)
A	51	16	7
B	10	12	5
C	37	64	68
D	2	7	20
Total	100	99	100
N	284	335	484

N	1,103	
NA on stratum	76	
Total N	1,179	

c. Plans for Graduate or Professional Study, Fall, 1961

Plans Index	Law-School Stratum		
	I (Per Cent)	II (Per Cent)	III (Per Cent)
Definitely attend, fall, 1961	95	86	72
Tentatively attend, fall, 1961	5	12	21
Definitely attend, future	0	2	7
Tentatively attend, future	0	0	0
Total	100	100	100
N	278	315	456

N	1,049	
Other plans	9	
NA on Plans Index	45	
NA on stratum	76	
Total N	1,179	

STRATUM, API, AND PROFESSIONAL STUDY

A combination of part-time work and part-time study is common in many of the fields of study entered by 1961 June graduates. But this pattern was not characteristic of the 1961 seniors who entered law school: in over nine cases out of ten, the law students carried a full course-load. Perhaps many students who enter law school without having completed college study law only part time, but that is clearly not the case here. Moreover, Table 5.3 shows that part-time study, such as it was, varied by API and type of law school attended. At each level of talent, the rate of full-time study declined with the lowering of institutional quality. However, the lowest rate of full-time study occurred among medium API students at Stratum II schools; yet, even in this group, 81 per cent carried a full course-load. On the other hand, none of the high API students at Stratum I schools was attending part time.

How did first-year law students evaluate their school experiences? The follow-up questionnaire included a number of items which respondents were asked to rate, including classroom teaching, caliber of students, faculty contacts, and the like. Responses to these items provide some insights into the process of legal education. In the row labeled "Total" at the bottom of parts *a–f* of Table 5.4 the percentages of students rating each of the six items as "excellent" or "good" are presented for the three law-school strata. With the exception of personal contacts with faculty, the first-year law students registered high levels of satisfaction with "caliber of classroom teaching," "curriculum and course offerings," "facilities and opportunities for research

Table 5.3 First-Year Law-School Course-Load, Law-School Stratum, and Academic Performance Index* (Per Cent Full-Time Study)

Academic Performance Index	Law-School Stratum		
	I (Per Cent)	II (Per Cent)	III (Per Cent)
High	100 (176)	96 (74)	93 (56)
Medium	98 (88)	93 (163)	81 (147)
Low	† (10)	88 (80)	91 (234)

N	1,028
NA on course-load	66
NA on API	9
NA on stratum	76
Total N	1,179

*Among men committed to law as college seniors and entering law school.
†Too few cases to percentage.

(including library)," "caliber of students," and "knowledge and professional standing of faculty." On the other hand, it appears that busy law-school professors were not sufficiently accessible to close to one-half of the students.

While the rating levels were uniformly high (faculty contacts

Table 5.4 Reactions to First Year of Law School, Law-School Stratum, and Academic Performance Index*

a. Per Cent Rating "Personal Contacts with Faculty" as "Excellent" or "Good"

Academic Performance Index	Law-School Stratum		
	I	II	III
High	36 (179)	40 (75)	59 (58)
Medium	28 (87)	48 (171)	49 (175)
Low	† (10)	46 (82)	60 (242)
Total	34 (276)	46 (328)	55 (475)

N	1,079
NA on reaction	15
NA on API	9
NA on stratum	76
Total N	1,179

b. Per Cent Rating "Caliber of Classroom Teaching" as "Excellent" or "Good"

Academic Performance Index	Law-School Stratum		
	I	II	III
High	97 (180)	88 (75)	62 (58)
Medium	97 (87)	94 (172)	75 (174)
Low	† (10)	90 (82)	78 (243)
Total	97 (277)	92 (329)	75 (475)

N	1,081
NA on reaction	13
NA on API	9
NA on stratum	76
Total N	1,179

*Among men committed to law as college seniors and entering law school.
†Too few cases to percentage.

(Table 5.4 continued)

Table 5.4 *Continued*

c. Per Cent Rating "Curriculum and Course Offerings"
as "Excellent" or "Good"

Academic Performance Index	Law-School Stratum		
	I	II	III
High	92 (179)	92 (75)	74 (58)
Medium	91 (87)	95 (172)	85 (174)
Low	† (10)	93 (82)	85 (243)
Total	92 (276)	94 (329)	84 (475)

N	1,080
NA on reaction	14
NA on API	9
NA on stratum	76
Total N	1,179

d. Per Cent Rating "Facilities and Opportunities for
Research (Including Library)" as "Excellent" or "Good"

Academic Performance Index	Law-School Stratum		
	I	II	III
High	94 (179)	84 (75)	74 (58)
Medium	92 (87)	91 (171)	69 (174)
Low	† (10)	90 (81)	73 (243)
Total	94 (276)	89 (327)	71 (475)

N	1,078
NA on reaction	16
NA on API	9
NA on stratum	76
Total N	1,179

†Too few cases to percentage.

aside), rates of endorsement for the remaining five aspects of professional training differed systematically among the strata: Stratum III students were somewhat less satisfied with their academic circumstances than were their fellow students in Stratum I and Stratum II. Assuming that institutional reputations depended in part upon student evaluations of the education received there, these findings lend additional support to the classification of law schools employed in this research.

Table 5.4 *Continued*

e. Per Cent Rating "Caliber of the Students" as "Excellent" or "Good"

Academic Performance Index	Law-School Stratum		
	I	II	III
High	97 (179)	80 (74)	52 (58)
Medium	100 (87)	89 (168)	63 (174)
Low	† (10)	89 (80)	69 (233)
Total	98 (276)	87 (322)	65 (465)

N	1,063
NA on reaction	31
NA on API	9
NA on stratum	76
Total N	1,179

f. Per Cent Rating "Knowledge and Professional Standing of the Faculty" as "Excellent" or "Good"

Academic Performance Index	Law-School Stratum		
	I	II	III
High	99 (179)	97 (75)	83 (58)
Medium	100 (87)	99 (170)	82 (173)
Low	† (10)	95 (81)	91 (242)
Total	100 (276)	98 (326)	87 (473)

N	1,075
NA on reaction	19
NA on API	9
NA on stratum	76
Total N	1,179

†Too few cases to percentage.

It comes as a distinct surprise to this former graduate student of sociology to discover that entering law students overwhelmingly endorse the caliber of classroom teaching to which they are exposed. Perhaps there are differences between graduate and professional training that impose different perspectives on this and other aspects of higher education. The question of access to faculty entails consideration of the time demands on faculty members for whom teaching, as such, is only one of the many roles typically attached to the position of "professor." It is noteworthy that only one in three students in the top eight schools considered their contacts with faculty as "excellent" or "good" in contrast with over one in two students enrolled in Stratum III law schools.

There are several interpretations possible, but the one amenable to empirical testing concerns the possibility that brighter students may be more demanding of their instructors than their fellow classmates. Because bright students in diverse law-school environments might have responded quite differently depending on where they are allocated, it is important to examine the joint effects of stratum and API if we are to understand why some students responded one way rather than another. Each part of Table 5.4 provides the requisite information.

Some 41 per cent of all high API students were satisfied with faculty contacts in contrast with 56 per cent of the low API students: satisfaction with faculty contacts is inversely related to academic performance. But high API students in Stratum III were far more likely to be satisfied than their counterparts who went to the top eight schools; indeed, they were as satisfied as the low API students in Stratum III, but for different reasons. It appears to be a problem of relative deprivation or relative gratification. In the competition for faculty recognition, high API students in the top eight were up against more formidable competition from their classmates, while the high API student attending a Stratum III school evidently had fewer classmates effectively vying for academic honors.

The relationships found for faculty reputation, facilities, and course offerings are quite different. Aside from personal contact with faculty, high API students in Stratum I law schools invariably were most likely to rate their first-year experiences as "excellent" or "good"; indeed, their judgments approach unanimity. High API students in the bottom stratum were least likely to register comparable levels of satisfaction. Consider, for example, student judgments of the caliber of classroom teaching (Table 5.4b). High API students in the aggregate were only slightly more satisfied with the quality of formal instruction than were the low API students (88 per cent as compared to 82 per cent). However, 97 per cent of the high API students in the top eight schools endorsed the caliber of teaching provided in the classroom in contrast with only 62 per cent of the students of equivalent undergraduate academic performance who entered Stratum III schools.

An analysis of the ratings of fellow students produces a similar outcome (Table 5.4*e*). Everyone in Stratum I judged his classmates to be of good or excellent legal timber, but only one-half of the high API students at the bottom thought as well of their fellows. Within each stratum, low API students were more satisfied with their classmates than were high API students. The interaction of student ability and institutional quality generated judgments ranging from 100 per cent endorsement of peers by students of medium API in Stratum I to 52 per cent endorsement by talented students in Stratum III. With minor variations, ratings on faculty reputations, course offerings, and research opportunities and facilities yield similar results (see Table 5.4*c–f*).

STRATUM, ACADEMIC PERFORMANCE INDEX, AND LAW-SCHOOL GRADES

Sociologists studying the legal profession give considerable attention to student perceptions of the social environment. Chances of a favorable assessment of the total learning situation in law school depend heavily on the interaction of personal ability and institutional quality, a finding of perhaps some interest to the professional law-school educator as well. It points to some of the environmental constraints on maintaining high levels of morale among students.

In the final analysis, however, the primary concern is performance: it is one of the facts of professional life that law-school grades are critically important for the entering law student determined to "succeed" in his profession—no matter how he defines success. The NORC follow-up survey provides information bearing on this vital topic. The spring, 1962, questionnaire asked: "What is your grade point average [GPA] so far in your post-bachelor's studies?" At the time they returned their completed questionnaires to NORC, some 80 per cent of the first-year law students were able to provide this information.

While the analysis could benefit from more definitive information, such as the final GPA for the first year of study, the materials that follow do not appear to be inadequate.

We shall first consider the relationship between API (which measures the four years of undergraduate work) and the spring, 1962, GPA in law school. Table 5.5 shows that among high API students, some 26 per cent secured grades of B+ or higher; only 6 per cent of the low API students reported comparable records. Not surprisingly, students who performed well in college were more likely to do better in law school than their medium or low API fellow students. Because we have shown that institutional quality is enormously varied, law-school GPA's probably deserve the same kind of statistical adjustment found necessary in the earlier NORC researches. An assessment of GPA for first-year study is possible by introducing stratum as a control variable. The results, shown in Table 5.6, indicate the following:

1. Reading down the table, it is evident that high API students were far more likely to report a GPA of B+ or better within each law school stratum than their fellow classmates who entered law school with a middle or low API. Furthermore, the high API student was twice as

Table 5.5 First-Year Law-School Grades and Academic Performance Index*

Academic Performance Index	Grades			Total (Per Cent)	Base N
	B+ or Higher (Per Cent)	B, B− (Per Cent)	C+ or Lower (Per Cent)		
High	26	41	33	100	243
Medium	13	34	53	100	354
Low	6	26	68	100	304

N	901
No grades yet	173
NA on grades	20
NA on API	9
NA on stratum	76
Total N	1,179

*Among men committed to law as college seniors and entering law school.

likely to report this GPA at a Stratum III school (41 per cent) than at a Stratum I school (21 per cent).

2. About four in ten high API students reported a B or B− GPA within each law-school stratum; one in three students of middling academic achievement in college now reported a similar GPA. Among low API students, the chances of making this GPA were somewhat better in Stratum III than in Stratum II. Even so, the second panel shows that within each stratum chances of reporting a B or B− were directly related to level of academic performance in college as was the case for those scoring B+ or higher.

3. Although they were among the top 20 per cent in the June, 1961, graduating class in academic performance, high API students are twice as likely to report a GPA of C+ or less if they are in Stratum I (39 per cent) than is the case in Stratum III (18 per cent). The competition in the top eight schools for high grades necessarily meant that some students are placed lower on the academic totem pole than would be

Table 5.6 First-Year Law-School Grades, Law-School Stratum, and Academic Performance Index*

Academic Performance Index	Law-School Stratum	Grades			Total (Per Cent)	Base N
		B+ or Higher (Per Cent)	B, B− (Per Cent)	C+ or Lower (Per Cent)		
High	I	21	40	39	100	124
	II	23	42	35	100	65
	III	41	41	18	100	54
Medium	I	6	32	62	100	65
	II	17	38	45	100	133
	III	13	32	55	100	156
Low	I	−	−	−	−	9†
	II	7	19	74	100	69
	III	5	28	66	99	226

N	901
No grades yet	173
NA on grades	20
NA on API	9
NA on stratum	76
Total N	1,179

*Among men committed to law as college seniors and entering law school.
†Too few cases to percentage.

their lot elsewhere. Within each stratum, a GPA of C+ or lower becomes increasingly frequent with each downward step in API.

In effect, GPA as reported by first-year law students reflected the interaction of academic ability and institutional quality. Thus performance in law school, like the perception of the academic environment of law school, represents an outcome shaped simultaneously by the student and his law school.

STRATUM, GPA, AND REACTIONS TO LEGAL STUDY

Let us now reconsider the findings on student ratings of several aspects of their study conditions. With the exception of ratings on contacts with faculty, we showed that stratum and API together had uniform effects on the ratings of the caliber of classroom teaching, etc., so that high API students in Stratum I were most likely to offer ratings of "excellent" or "good" while low API students in Stratum III were least likely to do so. The findings on faculty contacts indicated that the opposite relationship obtained: high API students in the top eight schools were least likely to be satisfied with faculty contacts. At this point, the data can be re-examined, starting with the premise that it is

Table 5.7 First-Year Law-School Grades, Law-School Stratum, and Rating of "Personal Contacts with Faculty"* (Per Cent "Excellent" or "Good")

Law-School Stratum	Grades		
	B+ or Higher	B, B—	C+ or Lower
I	53 (30)	35 (74)	38 (94)
II	55 (44)	51 (90)	38 (133)
III	66 (47)	61 (130)	53 (246)

N	888
NA and none yet on grades	181
NA on personal contacts	34
NA on stratum	76
Total N	1,179

*Among men committed to law as college seniors and entering law school.

not past performance that determines "access to faculty," but rather current performance.

As seen in Table 5.7, Stratum I students scoring B+ or higher were more likely than were the other students in that stratum to rate faculty contacts as "excellent" or "good." Nevertheless, when GPA was held constant, Stratum III students still rated faculty contacts as satisfactory more frequently than did students in Stratum II, who, in turn, were more satisfied than were their counterparts in the top eight schools. Two out of three B+ or better students at Stratum III schools gave this rating in contrast with only one out of three Stratum I students with GPA's of less than B+. With the exception of faculty contacts, ratings on the remaining aspects of the learning environment support the structure of relationships found when API was treated as the measure of talent.

6

Financial Support for Legal Education

Only a minority of the NORC sample of June, 1961, college graduates were planning to enter graduate or professional school in the fall of 1961. The graduating seniors among them who had chosen law as their future career were an exceptional group. An overwhelming majority said they would continue their studies in the fall, and, in fact, most of them did. In this chapter we describe their financial circumstances and indicate how law students entering the schools of differing strata were distributed in regard to stipend support and other sources of income during the academic year 1961–62. ("Stipend" is a generic term covering various kinds of financial support, including scholarships, fellowships, and teaching or research assistantships.) Of special interest are differences among stipend holders, stipend applicants who were unable to gain stipend support but nevertheless attended law school, and the remainder who attended but did not apply for a stipend.

In comparison with other fields, we know that law does rather badly in providing stipend support. The sciences and engineering give far more financial aid to their entering graduate students. Perhaps one reason for the discrepant levels of support is the different socio-economic composition of the various fields; law has the highest proportion of students coming from relatively affluent families. The question of "financial need" is a sticky one at best. Certainly, a policy of support for legal education would have to consider the overriding fact of the favorable situation of prospective lawyers. Beginning with this recognition, particular consideration would have to be given to the financial circumstances of law students, the distribution of stipend support among law schools, and how the available stipends are distributed among law students applying for such aid. Our data illuminate some of these questions.

STIPEND APPLICATIONS, TYPE OF ATTENDANCE IN 1961–62, AND API

Let us examine the rates of stipend application among students at different levels of academic performance who had definite plans for graduate or professional school in the fall of 1961 and their actual enrollment as reported in the one-year follow-up. Among those who went to law school, some 30 per cent had submitted applications at the time they returned the NORC questionnaire in the spring of 1961; of those who went on to graduate school, 25 per cent had made application; of those who planned to go on with their education immediately after college but did not, 22 per cent had sought stipends. Within each group of attenders and non-attenders, applications were made more frequently by high API students than by others (see Table 6.1).

Table 6.1 Stipend Application, Fall, 1961, Activity, and Academic Performance Index* (Per Cent Who Applied for a Stipend for Fall, 1961)

Fall, 1961, Activity	API			Total
	High	Medium	Low	
Law school	49 (320)	29 (433)	13 (321)	30 (1,075)
Graduate school	65 (20)	14 (36)	12 (32)	25 (88)
Not attending	50 (26)	31 (52)	8 (89)	22 (167)

N	1,329
NA on stipend application	8
NA on API	17
Not planning to attend, fall, 1961	343
Total N	1,697

*Among men committed to law as seniors and planning advanced study for fall, 1961.

Table 6.2 Reasons for Not Applying for a Stipend, Fall, 1961, Activity, and Academic Performance Index* (Per Cent Giving Each Reason)

Fall, 1961, Activity	Academic Performance Index	Reasons for Not Applying†							N
		Not Needed‡	Could Not Get§	Did Not Occur#	Too Little**	Was Not Going††	Duties‡‡	Other	
Law school	High	71	28	9	1	0	2	8	162
	Medium	44	48	6	4	1	1	7	304
	Low	37	55	7	2	1	1	12	274
Total		47	45	7	3	1	1	7	740
Graduate school	High	—	—	—	—	—	—	—	7§§
	Medium	42	42	3	3	3	0	6	29
	Low	43	50	7	4	4	0	7	28
Total		47	42	6	5	3	0	6	64
Not attending	High	—	—	—	—	—	—	—	12§§
	Medium	25	42	11	3	6	3	17	35
	Low	23	46	12	5	1	1	13	80
Total		25	42	11	5	5	2	14	127

N   931
NA on reasons   16
Application: "yes" and NA   390
NA on API   17
Not planning to attend, fall, 1961   343
Total N   1,697

*Among men committed to law as college seniors and planning advanced study for fall, 1961.

†Multiple responses were permitted.

‡I wouldn't need any support of this type.

§I didn't think I could get any.

#It didn't occur to me.

**The amount I could get would have been too little.

††I had no intention of going to school at the time applications were due.

Perhaps the crucial observation here is that the talented segment of those who planned to go on to professional school, who
applied for a stipend, but who nevertheless did not attend consists of a weighted sample of but fifteen students, or less than 1
per cent of the total sample of law aspirants.

In comparison with other career fields and fields of graduate
study, law aspirants had a low rate of stipend application. Why
did the others not bother to apply? Among those who entered law
school and graduate school, some 47 per cent said that they
"wouldn't need support of this type," and 25 per cent of the
attenders gave this reason as well (Table 6.2). Significantly, 71
per cent of the high API students in law school said that support
of this kind was not needed, and only 28 per cent circled "I
didn't think I could get any"; in contrast, 37 per cent of the low
API law students claimed that stipend support was unnecessary
and 55 per cent said they had no hopes of getting any. The high
API students who were in graduate school or out of school
completely during the academic year 1961–62 comprise too
small a group for additional analysis. However, over 40 per cent
of the graduate students who were below the high API group
said that there was no need for stipend support, and a similar
number felt they would not receive it even if they applied. The
overall impression is that the majority of those not applying for a
stipend simply did not require this form of assistance to imple-
ment their academic plans. This was especially true of the high
API students entering law schools.

The same point is made by examining the three variables —
law-school attendance, API, and reasons for not applying for a
stipend — from a related but different perspective. Table 6.3
shows that 86 per cent of the high API students and 77 per cent
of the low API students who said they did not need financial aid
were attending law school during the year following college
graduation. Among those who did not think they could get a
stipend, fully 94 per cent of the high API students were in law,
as were 75 per cent of their low API counterparts.

STIPEND HOLDING, API, AND LAW-SCHOOL STRATUM
How many law students held stipends during the first year of
academic study? The questionnaire item was phrased as follows:

During the academic year, did you receive a stipend (scholarship, fellowship, research or teaching assistantship) or similar financial aid?

The rate of stipend holding among the entering law students in the June, 1961, graduating class was 28 per cent. However, stipend holders were not randomly distributed among the entering law-school classes.

We will first consider the relationship of stipend holding, academic performance, and institutional quality without distinguishing for the moment between stipend applicants and others. Table 6.4a shows that stratum and API made a difference in the likelihood of holding any kind of stipend. Within each stratum, chances of getting stipends increased with API. Questions of financial need aside, talent apparently is rewarded. The rewards also depended on type of school attended. The young man of high API had a better chance of holding a stipend in Stratum III than in Stratum I; but, presumably, the competition was stiffer in the top eight schools. Interestingly enough, the low API student attending a Stratum II school was more likely to be holding a stipend than his counterpart in Stratum III.

If we consider the incidence of stipend holding among stipend applicants only, we find a different picture: in Stratum I stipend

Table 6.3 Reasons for Not Applying for a Stipend and Academic Performance Index* (Per Cent Attending Law School)

API	Reasons for Not Applying†	
	Not Needed‡	Could Not Get§
High	86 (126)	94 (48)
Medium	84 (158)	83 (174)
Low	77 (134)	75 (207)
Total	82 (418)	80 (429)

*Among men committed to law as college seniors and planning advanced study for fall, 1961.
†Multiple responses were permitted.
‡I wouldn't need any support of this type.
§I didn't think I could get any.

holding was directly related to talent; in Stratum II there were no API-related differences; and in Stratum III stipend holding was inversely related to talent so that low API applicants stood a better chance of holding a stipend than did the high API applicants! (see Table 6.4b). Furthermore, within each level of talent, stratum differences were such that the high API applicant was about equally likely to be holding a stipend no matter which type of school he attended, but the chances of obtaining a stipend increased with each step down the quality ladder if the student ranked below the top 20 per cent of the June, 1961, graduating class.

The same three variables appear in a different perspective in Table 6.4c. Here we see that the academic quality of students in the three stipend categories differed considerably when institutional quality was considered. At the one extreme, fully three-quarters of the stipend holders in Stratum I were high on API as compared with only one in twenty students of those who made no stipend application and then attended a Stratum III school. Furthermore, the academic caliber of stipend holders differed markedly by type of school, with the result that less than one in

Table 6.4 Stipend Holding (1961 – 62), Academic Performance Index, and Law-School Stratum*

a. Per Cent Holding Stipend among All Law-School Entrants

API	Law-School Stratum		
	I	II	III
High	33 (176)	46 (74)	49 (57)
Medium	20 (82)	29 (163)	25 (155)
Low	† (10)	31 (80)	15 (218)

N	1,015
NA on stipend	79
NA on API	9
NA on stratum	76
Total N	1,179

*Among men committed to law as college seniors and entering law school.
†Too few cases to percentage.

(Table 6.4 continued)

Table 6.4 *Continued*

---

b. Per Cent Holding Stipend, among Stipend Applicants Only

API	Law-School Stratum		
	I	II	III
High	65 (89)	71 (48)	68 (41)
Medium	52 (31)	71 (68)	72 (54)
Low	† (1)	68 (37)	80 (40)

N	409
Did not apply	606
NA on stipend	79
NA on API	9
NA on stratum	76
Total N	·1,179

---

c. Per Cent High on API

Law-School Stratum	Applied for Stipend		Did Not Apply
	Received	Did Not Receive	
I	78 (74)	66 (47)	59 (147)
II	32 (107)	30 (46)	16 (164)
III	28 (99)	36 (36)	5 (295)

N	1,015
NA on stipend	79
NA on API	9
NA on stratum	76
Total N	1,179

†Too few cases to percentage.

three stipend holders in Stratum III schools ranked high on API. Correlatively, the group turned down for stipends in Stratum III had a slightly higher proportion of high API students than did the group receiving stipend support.

One could infer from these tables that top national schools allocate stipends on the basis of talent while Stratum III schools do not consider talent as measured by API a relevant factor in determining who shall be awarded the available stipend support. The flaw of inference, of course, is that students who enrolled in Stratum III schools may have applied to and have been rejected by a law school in the other two strata. Possibly the Stratum III schools do not differentiate the value of the GPA's according to the quality of undergraduate school as the NORC researches have done in constructing the API. Hence they treat as superior those students whom the API indicates are nearer to being only average.

STRATUM, API, AND FAMILY INCOME

Perhaps financial aid is an intervening variable accounting for the realationship between stipend holding and academic performance as measured by the API. With family income as the indicator of need, the three variables of stratum, family income, and API together produce the pattern shown in Table 6.5.

In Stratum I the primary determinant of stipend holding was API; family income generated a secondary effect, with bright, "rich" applicants more likely to secure some form of stipend support than bright, "poor" applicants. Of course, both were far more likely to be holding a stipend than the applicants who did not rank high on API. In Stratum II, API again was more important than family income in determining who held a stipend.

Table 6.5 Academic Performance Index, Law-School Stratum, and Income of Parental Family (Per Cent Holding Stipends, among Stipend Applicants)*

Law-School Stratum	High API		Medium or Low API	
	$7,500 or More	Less Than $7,500	$7,500 or More	Less Than $7,500
I	69 (56)	57 (22)	37 (18)	† (7)
II	71 (26)	79 (13)	71 (68)	60 (27)
III	70 (67)	75 (15)	86 (52)	52 (30)

	N	401
	Did not apply	606
	NA on stipend	79
	NA on API/family income	17
	NA on stratum	76
	Total N	1,179

*Among men committed to law as college seniors and entering law school.
†Too few cases to percentage.

Unlike the pattern found in the top eight schools, stipends went more to the bright, "poor" applicants (79 per cent) among those who were not in the top 20 per cent of the graduating class. Among those scoring medium or low on API, the applicant of modest origin was less likely to have a stipend than was his more fortunate fellow applicant. Among those scoring high on API, the applicant of modest origin was somewhat more likely to receive a stipend than the one whose family had the higher income.

If talent and need are considered to be the crucial factors in allocating stipends, then the pattern of Stratum III is most unusual. There fully 86 per cent of the applicants who were both "rich" and "not bright" held stipends! The combination of money and lack of talent resulted in the highest rate of stipend holding found in the sample, while the same combination of attributes resulted in the lowest rate of stipend holding among Stratum I schools (37 per cent of the applicants). In Stratum II students low on both API and family income had the lowest rate of stipend holding.

The patterns of stipend holding among law students raise a number of questions: For example, why should the relationship between stipend holding and API be as varied and as unexpected as we have found it to be? But the data are limited; additional information would be required before we could begin to interpret the institutional functions of stipend giving in the field of legal education.

TYPES OF STIPENDS

What kinds of support did stipend holders receive for the study of law? Table 6.6 details the kind of support given to stipend recipients in the three strata of law schools. Most stipends in the field of legal education were scholarships that met some or all of the tuition costs. Some 80 per cent of the stipends awarded to students in Stratum I were of this kind; in Stratum III the proportion was slightly less (70 per cent). On the other hand, Stratum III recipients were more likely than were stipend holders in Stratum I to receive a scholarship or fellowship for tuition plus a cash grant (20 per cent as opposed to 12 per cent).

Almost all financial assistance offered to law students took one of these two forms; only a handful held teaching or research assistantships. In contrast, all June, 1961, graduating seniors holding stipends in a graduate or professional school received relatively less support in the form of scholarships or fellowships (55 per cent) and more aid in the form of duty stipends, i.e., teaching or research assistantships (40 per cent).

Furthermore, the value of all stipends received during the academic year varied by stratum, as seen in Table 6.7. Specifically, somewhat less than one-half of all stipends granted in Stratum I were worth less than $1,000 while close to four out of five stipends granted in Stratum III were below that figure. In fact, one out of five stipends held in both Strata II and III had a cash value of less than $200. In addition, the number of law students holding stipends of $2,000 or more was almost negligible. In contrast, the graduate and professional school cohort of June, 1961, college seniors fared rather well: some 40 per cent held stipends valued at $2,000 or more while only one-third received aid with a cash value of less than $1,000 (Miller, 1963, p. 79).

Table 6.6   Type of Stipend and Law-School Stratum*

Type of Stipend	Law-School Stratum		
	I (Per Cent)	II (Per Cent)	III (Per Cent)
Scholarship: tuition or less	81	72	70
Scholarship: tuition and cash	12	14	20
Teaching assistantship	0	2	1
Research assistantship	2	0	3
Other	4	12	6
Total	99	100	100
N	74	107	100

N	281
No stipend	743
NA on stipend	79
NA on stratum	76
Total N	1,179

*Among men committed to law school as college seniors and entering law school.

SOURCES OF INCOME BY STIPEND CATEGORY

Since the monetary value of stipends held by law students is relatively low, stipend holders as well as other students clearly relied on other forms of support. Table 6.8 shows the frequency with which stipend holders, applicants who failed to secure stipends, and non-applicants in the three law-school strata secured significant financial support. For this purpose, it was asked from what source or sources the student received the sum of $200 or more. In every stratum students relied on parents. However, students in each stipend category were less likely to rely on parents as a source of support with each step down the institutional ladder. On the one hand, nine out of ten non-stipend holders in Stratum I relied on parents or relatives; on the other, only one out of two stipend holders in Stratum III was supported by parents or relatives.

Non-applicants in each stratum were equally likely to report withdrawal of savings (one out of three did). Stratum III stipend holders and applicants who did not secure stipends were less

Table 6.7 Value of Stipend and Law-School Stratum*

Value of Stipend	Law-School Stratum		
	I (Per Cent)	II (Per Cent)	III (Per Cent)
Less than $200	8	20	20
$200 – $499	18	29	24
$500 – $999	18	21	35
$1,000 – $1,499	42	16	15
$1,500 – $1,999	9	7	1
$2,000 – $2,499	3	4	0
$2,500 or more	1	3	4
Total	99	100	99
N	74	107	98

N	279
No stipend	743
NA on stipend	81
NA on stratum	76
Total N	1,179

*Among men committed to law as college seniors and entering law school.

likely to rely on savings than were those in Stratum I. Furthermore, stipend holders in every stratum were more likely to take loans than those who did not apply for a stipend. The likelihood of loans increased among stipend holders with each step up the quality ladder; applicants *not* receiving a stipend in Strata I and II also took loans more frequently than their counterparts in Stratum II.

The most important source of income for many law students was employment. In Table 6.9, part-time and full-time employment rates are shown by stratum. Not surprisingly, students who were unsuccessful in obtaining stipends were most likely to be employed; the rates of employment among students ranged from 21 per cent at the top eight schools to 81 per cent at the bottom schools.

Rates of employment varied considerably by stipend category and by stratum. In each instance, students in Stratum I were

Table 6.8 Source of Non-Stipend Income ($200 or More), Law-School Stratum, and Stipend Holding*

Per Cent Receiving $200 or More From	Law-School Stratum	Applied for Stipend		Did Not Apply
		Received	Did Not Receive	
Parents	I	77 (73)	91 (47)	90 (148)
	II	68 (107)	64 (50)	74 (165)
	III	52 (99)	51 (37)	66 (293)
Savings	I	56†	74	35
	II	41	42	35
	III	34	16	37
Loan	I	41	28	4
	II	35	36	18
	III	23	11	10
	N	1,019		
	NA on sources	5		
	NA on stipend	79		
	NA on stratum	76		
	Total N	1,179		

*Among men committed to law as college seniors and entering law school.

†The percentages reporting $200 or more from these sources (parents, savings, loans) are based on the N's shown in the first panel. A similar format is used in Tables 6.10, 6.12, and 7.1.

less likely to be employed full time than those in Stratum III. In addition, when stipend recipients and other stipend applicants were employed, their employment was more likely to be part time than was the case among their counterparts who did not apply for assistance. At the one extreme, *all* the stipend holders and other applicants in the top eight who worked had part-time jobs, while just over one-half of the non-applicants in Stratum III worked only part time.

NON-STIPEND MONTHLY INCOME

The average monthly incomes (before taxes and deductions) derived from the sources upon which law students drew to meet

Table 6.9 Employment, Law-School Stratum, and Stipend Holding*

a. Per Cent Employed

Law-School Stratum	Applied for Stipend		Did Not Apply
	Received	Did Not Receive	
I	19 (74)	21 (47)	13 (145)
II	34 (107)	52 (50)	41 (165)
III	48 (100)	81 (37)	41 (296)

N = 1,024

b. Per Cent Employed Part Time (among Those Employed)

Law-School Stratum	Applied for Stipend		Did Not Apply
	Received	Did Not Receive	
I	100 (14)	100 (10)	74 (19)
II	86 (35)	65 (26)	60 (68)
III	65 (48)	77 (30)	53 (120)

N	370
Not employed	654
NA on stipend	79
NA on stratum	76
Total N	1,179

*Among men committed to law as college seniors and entering law school.

their expenses are shown in Table 6.10. The upper panel shows the proportion of students in each stipend category (by stratum) who had no monthly income. Among stipend holders, the likelihood of having no additional income declined with each step down the institutional ladder: two out of five stipend holders in the top eight schools apparently relied solely on their stipends. Furthermore, applicants who failed to secure assistance and non-applicants in Stratum I were also more likely than were their counterparts attending Stratum III schools to report that they had no monthly income.

The next panel shows the proportion reporting less than $200 monthly in current average non-stipend income. Stipend holding and stratum are both involved; two-thirds of the stipend holders in Stratum I are in this category, in contrast to 31 per cent of those Stratum III students who were not given assistance and 41 per cent of the non-applicants in Stratum III. This pattern is related to the frequency and kind of employment. For example, because of the high rate of full-time employment among non-

Table 6.10 Non-Stipend Income, Law-School Stratum, and Stipend Holding*

Income	Law-School Stratum	Applied for Stipend		Did Not Apply
		Received	Did Not Receive	
Per cent no monthly income	I	39 (49)	21 (34)	31 (104)
	II	36 (73)	30 (30)	20 (104)
	III	21 (62)	7 (29)	24 (192)
Per cent less than $200	I	67†	68	58
	II	60	50	46
	III	52	31	41

N	677
NA on income	347
NA on stipend	79
NA on stratum	76
Total N	1,179

*Among men committed to law as college seniors and entering law school.
†See footnote to Table 6.8.

Table 6.11 Non-Stipend Income, Law-School Stratum, and Stipend Holding*

Law-School Stratum	Stipend Holding	Monthly Income						Total (Per Cent)	Base N
		None (Per Cent)	$1–$199 (Per Cent)	$200–$299 (Per Cent)	$300–$399 (Per Cent)	$400–$599 (Per Cent)	$600 and Over (Per Cent)		
I	Applied, received	39	29	8	8	16	0	100	49
	Applied, not received	21	47	18	9	6	0	101	34
	Did not apply	31	27	6	16	15	5	100	104
II	Applied, received	36	25	14	7	15	4	101	73
	Applied, not received	30	20	17	13	17	3	100	30
	Did not apply	20	26	14	13	19	8	100	104
III	Applied, received	21	31	13	9	17	9	100	62
	Applied, not received	7	24	21	24	17	7	100	29
	Did not apply	23	18	15	18	18	6	98	192

N 677
NA on income 347
NA on stipend 79
NA on stratum 76
Total N 1,179

*Among men committed to law as college seniors and entering law school.

stipend holders in Stratum III, 15 per cent report monthly incomes of $200 – $299; 18 per cent report $300 – $399; another 18 per cent estimate between $400 and $599; and 6 per cent report even higher monthly incomes (Table 6.11).

DEBTS AND POSTGRADUATE STUDY

Another little-known aspect of the financial circumstances of students enrolled in the study of law is the amount of debt they incur for their studies. The NORC survey provides this kind of information on the basis of responses to the following question:

Considering money borrowed for education (tuition, living expenses while in school, books, etc.) . . . how much money have you borrowed for postgraduate studies?

In the upper panel of Table 6.12 proportions of students in each stratum and stipend category who circled "None" are presented. Among stipend holders, absence of debt increased with each step down the stratum ladder. Stipend holders in the top eight schools were especially likely to incur debt to meet

Table 6.12 Debts for Postgraduate Study, Law-School Stratum, and Stipend Holding*

Amount of Debt	Law-School Stratum	Applied for Stipend		Did Not Apply
		Received	Did Not Receive	
Per cent None	I	54 (72)	65 (43)	86 (144)
	II	62 (107)	58 (50)	78 (158)
	III	74 (97)	92 (36)	81 (286)
Per cent $500 or more	I	28†	21	9
	II	26	36	11
	III	20	6	13

N	993
NA on debt	31
NA on stipend	79
NA on stratum	76
Total N	1,179

*Among men committed to law as college seniors and entering law school.
†See footnote to Table 6.8.

academic expenses. Of those applicants who failed to secure stipends, those located in Stratum III were again most likely to be free of debt for postgraduate study. Among students who did not apply for stipends there were no strong differences by stratum—nearly all were debt free. The table also shows that stipend holders invariably were less likely to be free of this kind of debt within each stratum than were the non-applicants.

In the lower panel of Table 6.12 rates of indebtedness totaling $500 or more are presented. Non-applicants in Stratum I and applicants unable to secure stipends in Stratum III were least likely to be in debt for this amount, but for different reasons. The former category comprised students who were likely to be in favorable socio-economic circumstances, while the latter were engaged in full-time or part-time employment.

ASSETS OF LAW STUDENTS

Just as information is needed on the amount of debt that law students incur for their postgraduate study, so is there need for estimates of assets that students have access to in the face of emergencies and the like. Table 6.13 shows the frequency with which students in the several stipend categories reported their assets in the form of savings or securities (or other assets that

Table 6.13 Total Liquid Assets, Law-School Stratum, and Stipend Holding* (Per Cent Having $1,000 or More)

Law-School Stratum	Applied for Stipend		Did Not Apply
	Received	Did Not Receive	
I	38 (72)	51 (45)	64 (142)
II	31 (104)	33 (48)	54 (160)
III	47 (97)	38 (34)	50 (287)

N	989
NA on assets	35
NA on stipend	79
NA on stratum	76
Total N	1,179

*Among men committed to law as college seniors and entering law school.

could be converted into cash) totaling $1,000 or more. Sixty-four per cent of the students in Stratum I who did not apply for stipends estimated their assets at this figure or above, while only 38 per cent of the stipend holders in that stratum were likely to be at this level. The Stratum III group of stipend holders most frequently gave an estimate of $1,000 or more. In Stratum II only one out of three of all stipend applicants, both those holding stipends and the others, possessed assets amounting to this figure, while more than one-half of the non-applicants in that stratum did so. Stipend holders in Stratum III somewhat more frequently reported assets of at least $1,000 than did the applicants who failed to obtain stipends.

STIPENDS AND GRADES

Having documented the level of stipend holding among students attending law school, the distribution of stipends among the several types of schools, the other sources of support for students with different stipend experiences, and their debts and assets, it remains to be seen whether there is a distinctive "payoff" at the completion of the first year of study. Table 6.14*a* presents the proportion of students who reported GPA's of B+ or better at the time they returned their completed questionnaires, considering law-school stratum and stipend category. The table shows a weak but systematic relationship. In each stratum the stipend holders were slightly more likely to indicate GPA's of B+ or better than were the non-applicants. In view of the irregular relationships found earlier between stipend holding and API, the table is interesting not because the relationship is so weak, but rather because it exists at all.

A different but related question can be put to the same data: How many students classified by their current GPA held stipends in the three strata of law schools? Table 6.14*b* shows that the differences in stipend holding between Stratum I students who scored B+ or better and those who scored C+ or lower are negligible. However, in the remaining strata students scoring B+ or better were more likely to hold stipends (50 per cent in Stratum II), in contrast with students who maintained a GPA of C+ or less (30 per cent in Stratum II).

Table 6.14 Grade Point Average (First Year of Law School), Law-School Stratum, and Stipend Holding*

a. Per Cent Reporting B+ or Higher

Law-School Stratum	Applied for Stipend		Did Not Apply
	Received	Did Not Receive	
I	17 (54)	18 (33)	13 (104)
II	24 (93)	17 (41)	13 (128)
III	18 (98)	12 (33)	10 (272)

b. Per Cent Holding Stipend

Law-School Stratum	GPA		
	B+ or Higher	B, B—	C+ or Lower
I	31 (29)	32 (70)	25 (92)
II	50 (44)	36 (88)	30 (130)
III	37 (49)	28 (127)	18 (227)

N	856
NA on grades	9
No grades yet	159
NA on stipend	79
NA on stratum	76
Total N	1,179

*Among men committed to law as college seniors and entering law school.

Table 6.15 Stipend for Second Year of Legal Study (1962–63), Law-School Stratum, and Grade Point Average (First Year of Law School)* (Per Cent Having Stipend for 1961–63)

Law-School Stratum	GPA		
	B+ or Higher	B, B—	C+ or Lower
I	28 (29)	28 (68)	12 (89)
II	36 (42)	26 (85)	21 (129)
III	22 (54)	16 (117)	9 (234)

N	847
NA on 1963 stipend	68
NA on grades and none yet	188
NA on stratum	76
Total N	1,179

*Among men committed to law as college seniors and entering law school.

Furthermore, Table 6.15 indicates that performance in the first year of legal study, as measured by the reported GPA, did make a difference in stipend holding for the following year (academic year 1962–63). In Stratum I students who scored C+ or less were one-half as likely to obtain stipend assistance (mostly in the form of tuition scholarships) than were students with a higher GPA. Similar relationships were found in the remaining strata. The results in this table must be considered provisional, since their information on the acceptance of stipends for the next academic year is derived from questionnaires which were completed in the spring and summer of 1962, before the next academic year actually began.

7

Academic
Plans and Employment
Expectations

Two topics are considered in this last chapter. The first is the continuity of professional study — how many students planned to continue their law study in the academic year 1962–63? How many 1961 college seniors planning on a career in law dropped out of school after their first year of legal study? The second topic is the employment preferences of law-school students. What kind of practice did various students expect to have?

ACADEMIC PLANS FOR 1962–63

On the face of it, the question of continuity of legal study and dropout from law school would seem to be an intriguing problem deserving considerable attention. Whether or not law students were planning to continue their professional study could be ascertained from responses to the following question.

Indicate your plans for the coming (1962–63) academic year by circling one of the following:
  Will continue studies in
    Same field, same school
    Same field, but different school
    Same school, but different field
    Different field and different school
  Will not be enrolled because
    Work for degree will be completed
    Studying in absentia
    Interrupting my studies temporarily
    Quitting my studies short of the degree

That this is definitely *not* a "problem" for the law-school group that is the subject of this report is indicated in Table 7.1. The overwhelming majority (more than nine out of ten) plan to continue their studies in the field of law. This unusually low rate of attrition is understandable if we consider that our law aspirants have successfully survived four years of undergraduate training in American colleges of arts and science prior to their legal study. It would appear that the entering law students who have gone to law school without completing college, and perhaps the midyear graduate or the student entering law school after a time gap of one or more years after graduating from college, represent the prime risks for dropout.

But what can we learn about the almost two in twenty in our group who did not continue in law school? There were both institutional and academic performance differentials in dropout rates. Not only did top students in top law schools invariably

Table 7.1 Plans for Second-Year Legal Study, Law-School Stratum, and Grade Point Average (First Year of Law School)*

		GPA		
Plans	Law-School Stratum	B+ or Higher (Per Cent)	B, B− (Per Cent)	C+ or Lower (Per Cent)
Continue legal study at same school	I	100 (30)	99 (74)	84 (95)
	II	93 (44)	97 (90)	84 (132)
	III	89 (55)	88 (134)	85 (248)
Continue legal study at different school	I	0†	0	4
	II	5	2	6
	III	9	4	2
Discontinue legal study	I	0	1	12
	II	2	1	10
	III	2	8	13

N	902
NA on grades, and no grades yet	201
NA on stratum	76
Total N	1,179

*Among men committed to law as college seniors and entering law school.
†See footnote to Table 6.8.

plan to continue their study of law into the second year, but they planned to do so at the same school.

At the one extreme, all Stratum I students reporting a GPA of B+ or higher planned to continue into the second year at the same law school. Among Stratum III students doing as well academically, 89 per cent had identical academic plans for 1962–63 and 85 per cent of the students reporting GPA's of C+ or lower reported this intention. In addition, Table 7.1 shows that there were institutionally linked differences on plans for transferring to a different law school. In Stratum I a handful of students who did relatively poorly in their academic work intended to change schools; in Stratum II both the better students (B+ or higher) and the poorer students (C+ or lower) planned to shift schools; among students in Stratum III, 9 per cent of the superior students intended to study law in a different school setting. It would be instructive to know whether a change in law-school affiliation entails a change in stratum.

Among those who did not plan to enroll in 1962–63, the major reasons were "quitting my studies short of the degree" and "interrupting my studies temporarily." Whether the drop-outs who gave the latter reason will later return to law school could be determined in the course of a follow-up survey.

The major conclusion of this brief discussion of the academic plans of first-year law students in our sample is that the dropout problem is negligible at the end of the first year of professional study. It would appear that grades achieved during the first year accounted for most of the attrition of those who did not plan to continue their study of law. If a student in Stratum I or II performed well or reasonably well during the first year of professional study, there was virtually no chance that he would abandon his law course. However, if he did well in his work at a Stratum III law school, there was a discernible tendency to seek the remainder of his training at a different school.

EMPLOYMENT EXPECTATIONS

With the exception of Lortie's work (1958) there is no documentation on the molding of preferences among law students for one rather than another type of law practice. There is little that indicates whether such preferences and expectations are altered in the course of professional training or whether these orientations have a role in channeling the neophyte lawyer into solo practice, professional partnership, corporations, or government.

The expectations of students at the end of their first year of law school remained pretty much uncrystallized (Table 7.2).[1] On a multiple-response question concerning long-term employment, about seven out of ten mentioned professional partnerships as a form of long-term career employment, but over four in ten (43 per cent) also mentioned "self-employment or a family-owned business." Unfortunately, the latter item confounded two distinctive routes: that of the solo practitioner who plans to go it alone, and that of the lawyer-businessman. Close to one in four students (24 per cent) considered the federal government as a potential employer, and another 13 per cent circled "state or local government." Employment with a private company having 100 employees or more was indicated by 14 per cent, and just under one in ten also indicated that they were considering career employment with a small private company, i.e., employing

[1]About one-half of the students selected only one of the organizational contexts potentially available, while the remainder selected two or more. Professional partnership was the sole choice of 28 per cent of the sample, 6 per cent endorsed government as their one and only objective, and 16 per cent said they expected to be self-employed or work in the family business.

Table 7.2 Employment Expectations of First-Year Law Students*

Long-Term Career Employment	Per Cent
Professional partnerships	70
Self-employed or family business	43
Federal government	24
State or local government	13
Private company with 100 employees or more	14
Private company with less than 100 employees	9
College or university	4
All other	5
Total	182

N	1,115	
NA on expected employment	64	
Total N	1,179	

*Among men committed to law as college seniors and entering law school.

less than one hundred persons. While the great majority thought of professional partnerships, clearly a variety of work settings was considered by these first-year law students.

ALTERNATIVE CAREER ROUTES

If a key dimension of intra-occupational differentiation is provided by the organizational context of professional practice, then the distinctive modes of occupational integration afforded the legal profession should be mirrored in the varieties of long-term career employment expected by these students. Professional partnership and government employment are the poles; the former presumably embodies the traditional ideal of legal professionalism, while the latter involves maximum engagement in a large bureaucracy. However, because of the high intellectual and professional standards traditionally associated with employment by the federal government (at least in the younger years of practice), a large firm partnership and federal employment may approximate each other in prestige.

Because lawyers are likely to move back and forth from the public to the private aspects of practice, we asked whether at the end of the first year of law study there were distinctive differences among those anticipating partnerships only, government only, both professional partnerships and government, or neither.

LAW STRATUM AND EXPECTED WORK SETTING

Table 7.3 shows that students variously located among the law schools in the United States differed in the frequency with which they selected these patterns of employment. Approximately one out of every two students in each stratum expected partnerships only, but the likelihood that a student would consider both government and partnerships lessened with the lowering of law-school quality. In contrast, Stratum I students were slightly less likely than students in the remaining strata to make choices other than government or partnerships.

LAW STRATUM AND RELIGIOUS ORIGINS

Within each stratum, furthermore, there were distinctive differences when the religious origins of the first-year law students were considered. The upper panel of Table 7.4 demonstrates the patterns in Stratum I: Protestants were most likely to expect only partnerships (68 per cent), while Jews were least likely to do so (38 per cent). On the other hand, Jews were most likely to list government as their only current choice (12 per cent), while Catholics and Jews were twice as likely as Protestants to consider other channels. These findings further refine some of the observations on the consequences of allocation in Chapter 4.

In Stratum II, however, Jews listed partnerships more frequently than did Protestants or Catholics, but they less often said "government only" or other career channels. In contrast, Catholics more frequently considered both possibilities and Protestants overchose "government only" (see the middle panel of Table 7.4). Yet another religious pattern emerged from Stratum III schools: the lower panel of the same table shows that Catholics were underrepresented among those expecting professional partnerships only, while Jews and Protestants demonstrated profiles of choice that were essentially similar. Clearly, conceptions of contexts for professional practice among first-year law students depended on religious origins as well as on the type of law school attended.

Table 7.3 Law-School Stratum and Expected Work Setting*

Expected Work Setting	Law-School Stratum		
	I (Per Cent)	II (Per Cent)	III (Per Cent)
Professional partnership	53	45	50
Government	6	7	9
Both	25	20	16
Other	16	28	25
Total	100	100	100
N	275	317	442

N	1,034
NA on parent's occupation	69
NA on stratum	76
Total N	1,179

*Among men committed to law as college seniors and entering law school.

STRATUM AND FATHER'S OCCUPATION

We know that access to parts of the metropolitan bar depends in large part on a man's social and academic credentials. In addition to the appropriate religious origins, there is evidence that the "proper" social class background is a decisive advantage in making one's way in the legal profession. Using the household head's occupation as the indicator of social class origins, Table 7.5 shows the structure of expectations among students classified by occupational level in the several law-school strata. The upper panel shows that students in the top eight schools

Table 7.4 Religious Origins, Law-School Stratum, and Expected Work Setting*

Law-School Stratum	Expected Work Setting	Original Religion		
		Protestant (Per Cent)	Catholic (Per Cent)	Jewish (Per Cent)
I	Professional partnership	64	47	38
	Both	23	22	29
	Government	3	2	12
	Other	11	30	21
Total		101	101	100
N		132	60	84
II	Professional partnership	43	42	60
	Both	18	23	18
	Government	10	7	3
	Other	29	28	19
Total		100	100	100
N		128	138	57
III	Professional partnership	55	37	57
	Both	15	21	13
	Government	9	12	6
	Other	21	31	24
Total		100	101	100
N		205	160	107

N	1,071
NA on religion	32
NA on stratum	76
Total N	1,179

*Among men committed to law as college seniors and entering law school.

whose fathers were in blue-collar occupations split their choices between partnerships and the combination of government and partnerships as the anticipated locus of employment; they showed no interest in government as the only career route and only a handful considered other contexts. In contrast, the majority of students with white-collar origins opted for partnerships. Consequently, fewer considered the double choice and

Table 7.5 Parent's Occupation, Law-School Stratum, and Expected Work Setting*

Law-School Stratum	Expected Work Setting	Parent's Occupation		
		Professional (Per Cent)	Other White Collar (Per Cent)	Blue Collar (Per Cent)
I	Professional partnership	52	59	44
	Both	26	19	44
	Government	4	9	0
	Other	18	13	12
Total		100	100	100
N		129	121	25
II	Professional partnership	57	41	33
	Both	16	24	22
	Government	5	7	16
	Other	22	28	29
Total		100	100	100
N		122	140	55
III	Professional partnership	52	42	54
	Both	15	14	17
	Government	8	9	10
	Other	25	35	19
Total		100	100	100
N		128	224	90

N	1,034
NA on parent's occupation	69
NA on stratum	76
Total N	1,179

*Among men committed to law as college seniors and entering law school.

some indicated government only. Government is the destination of many lower-class law students, but it is interesting to note that the small group of blue-collar students who made it to the top eight law schools simply did not consider this as their one and only destination.

Within Stratum II the social character of organizational preferences was systematic: professional partnerships varied directly with occupational level; choice of government only was inversely related to occupational level; the dual choice also became a more frequent pattern of selection in schools located in Strata II and III than among the top eight.

The lower panel of the table shows that students of white-collar, but not professional, occupational origins underchose professional partnerships and most frequently anticipated employment settings other than partnerships or government. There is some indication (not shown in this table) that prospective lawyers of lower-middle-class origins were intending to become businessmen-lawyers. In effect, students from professional families considered partnerships, regardless of the type of law school they attended. However, as we have seen, the type of law school did have an impact on the expectations of other white- and blue-collar families.

STRATUM AND TALENT

The question of talent, as measured by any of a variety of indicators, clearly should be considered as well as "lineage." In the next wave of NORC's longitudinal study, it will be useful to learn who among our group was appointed to the school's law review, how they fared in terms of grades, and the like. In the meantime, our most comprehensive measure of performance is provided by the API. Table 7.6 shows the choices by stratum and API.

Students in Stratum I with high API were more likely to expect partnerships and less likely to aim for government. In Stratum II the same outcomes were found. With each step down in talent as measured by the undergraduate record, the likelihood of considering partnerships or the combination of government and partnerships declined, while the choices of government only and other forms of professional practice were more common among the low API group in Stratum II than among their abler counterparts. Stratum III presents still another picture. Again, API predicts partnerships only and other career channels; on the other hand, high API students in this bottom stratum were also more likely to opt for government only while none of them considered both avenues simultaneously.

Table 7.6 Academic Performance Index, Law-School Stratum, and Expected Work Setting*

Law-School Stratum	Expected Work Setting	Academic Performance Index		
		High (Per Cent)	Medium (Per Cent)	Low (Per Cent)
I	Professional partnership	57	47	—
	Both	23	28	—
	Government	3	12	—
	Other	17	13	—
Total		100	100	—
N		180	93	10†
II	Professional partnership	49	49	37
	Both	25	19	18
	Government	7	5	15
	Other	20	28	30
Total		101	101	100
N		76	172	82
III	Professional partnership	72	50	43
	Both	0	11	21
	Government	14	12	9
	Other	14	28	26
Total		100	101	99
N		58	177	246

N	1,094
NA on API	9
NA on stratum	76
	1,179

*Among men committed to law as college seniors and entering law school.
†Too few cases to percentage.

EMPLOYMENT SETTINGS AND OCCUPATIONAL VALUES

While a large-scale survey would hardly be considered the ideal vehicle for obtaining personality measures, indicators of occupational values taken from sample surveys have been effectively employed in research on occupational choice. A substantial body of research points to the integration of personal values and occupational choice. Davis (1965), for example, has shown that in comparison with other career fields, graduating seniors who chose law tended to endorse the values of "making a lot of money" and "opportunities to work with people rather than things." Similarly, students expecting long-term career employment in the form of professional partnerships or government should shift values over a period of time in order to arrive at a consonance of values and expected work setting.

Can it be that once the occupational choice has been determined the organizational context in which the occupation is carried on takes precedence over occupational values? One of the merits of a longitudinal study is that it provides provisional answers for precisely this kind of question.

In the remainder of this chapter we consider the expected work setting together with the endorsement of occupational values of the entire sample of first-year law students at two points in time. Specifically, we trace the changes in rate of endorsement of an occupational value ("slow but steady progress") and an expected work setting (government) as the students moved from college graduation through the first year of professional study. In this analysis the assumption is that students were consistent when they expected government employment and endorsed the value of "slow but steady progress."[2] The data are presented in Table 7.7 and show the following:

1. *Initial consistency.* — There was a modest relationship between work setting and occupational values among graduating seniors. Sixty-two per cent chose government as a long-term employer and endorsed "slow but steady progress," or chose an employer other than government and did not endorse this occupational value.

[2]The analysis closely follows the approach outlined by Barton and Lazarsfeld (1962).

Table 7.7 Occupational Values and Expectations of Work Settings among First-Year Law Students at Two Points in Time

Choices One Year Later (1962)	Choices as Graduating Seniors (June, 1961)				
	Security-Oriented Employment Security-Oriented Values (Per Cent)	Security-Oriented Employment Not Security-Oriented Values (Per Cent)	Not Security-Oriented Employment Security-Oriented Values (Per Cent)	Not Security-Oriented Employment Not Security-Oriented Values (Per Cent)	Totals (Spring, 1962) (Per Cent)
Security-oriented employment* Security-oriented values†	Remain consistent 0.5	Become consistent 2.4	3.1	Consistent change 1.3	7.3
Security-oriented employment Not security-oriented values‡	Become inconsistent 0.5	Remain inconsistent 7.5	2.7	Become inconsistent 9.4	20.1
Not security-oriented employment§ Security-oriented values	1.2	2.4	3.4	7.6	14.6
Not security-oriented employment Not security-oriented values	Consistent change 1.2	Become consistent 12.6	3.9	Remain consistent 40.3	58.0
Spring, 1961, totals	3.4	24.9	13.1	58.6	100.0

N   1,079
NA on values   100
Total N   1,179

*Security-oriented employment = government.
†Security-oriented values = "slow but steady progress."
‡Not security-oriented values = does not endorse "slow but steady progress."
§Not security-oriented employment = other than government.

2. *Trends in choice of values and work settings.* — There was almost no change among the group of first-year students during the year intervening between graduation and the completion of one year of legal study. The proportion expecting to be employed by government declined slightly from 28 to 27 per cent; the percentage endorsing "slow but steady progress" increased from 18 to 22 per cent.

3. *Turnover in choice of government and importance of "security."* — Despite the surface stability, there was considerable individual change in both directions. Eight per cent changed both values and choice of setting; 40 per cent changed one of them; only 52 per cent remained exactly as they had been one year earlier vis-à-vis the relative importance of security and the expectation of working (or not working) in a government setting.

4. *Trend toward consistency.* — There was a slight increase in consistency of choice of work setting and occupational values after one year of legal study. One year later, graduating seniors who attended a law school tended to integrate their job expectation and their occupational values; 65 per cent chose consistently as against an earlier 62 per cent.

5. *Turnover of consistency.* — The 3 per cent net gain in consistency was the result of fairly large countermovements. Twenty-two per cent moved from "inconsistent" to "consistent," while 19 per cent moved the other way.

6. *The relative strength of the job context and the occupational value.* — Those who moved toward consistency did so less frequently by changing their occupational value to conform to their work-setting preference (6 per cent) than by changing their expected work setting to conform to their values (16 per cent). Among those who became inconsistent, 8 per cent did so through a change in values, while 11 per cent did the reverse.

In the aggregate, first-year law students moved in the direction of consistency of values and career expectations but the aggregate measure of consistency conceals the shuffling of almost one-half of the students from one stance on value and/or organizational settings to another. Crucial to the question of the relative potency of values and anticipated work settings is the finding that when movements in the direction of consistency did occur, first-year law students more often switched their destinations to conform to their occupational values than vice versa.

Whether the pattern persists through the second and third years of legal study remains to be seen; and more importantly, whether these preferences have any bearing on the employment secured after leaving school would be an important focus for additional study.

Appendix 1

Spring, 1961 Questionnaire College Career Plans

NATIONAL OPINION RESEARCH CENTER

University of Chicago
5720 Woodlawn Avenue, Chicago 37, Illinois

Dear Student: April, 1961

National Opinion Research Center, a non-profit research organization affiliated with the University of Chicago, has been asked by three Federal agencies, the U.S. Office of Education, The National Science Foundation, and the National Institutes of Health, to survey the career plans of seniors in American colleges and universities.

You are one of 40,000 students in 135 schools who have been chosen by scientific probability sampling methods to participate in this study.

The research is designed to yield important information on the relationships between college experiences and career plans.

The questionnaire requires 30 minutes or so to fill out. Please answer the questions as frankly and accurately as you can. Your answers will be absolutely confidential, and no individual student's answers will be revealed in the reports, which will be based on statistical tabulations.

Almost all of the questions can be answered by drawing a circle around one or more numbers or letters in the right hand margins of the questionnaire. Thus:

I am now— (Circle one.)
A student in high school   1
A student in college   ②
A student in graduate or
    professional school   x

NOTE: After each question there are instructions in parentheses. Please follow these instructions closely as they are very important for data processing.

A. If it says "(Circle one.)," draw a circle around only the one number or letter which *best describes* your answer, even though one or more other alternatives might be relevant.

B. If it says "(Circle one in each column.)" or "(Circle one in each row.)," please look to see that you have circled one and only one number or letter in each of the appropriate rows or columns.

C. If it says "(Circle as many as apply.)," circle as many or as few numbers or letters in the columns or rows as you think are relevant.

If you are interested in the results of this study, please write a letter or card requesting a copy of the results to National Opinion Research Center, 5720 South Woodlawn, Chicago 37, Illinois, *after October, 1961.*

Thank you very much for your help.

Sincerely,

James A. Davis
Study Director

Survey 431

I. PLANS FOR THIS COMING FALL

1. What will you be doing this Fall?

Circle the number which describes what you will be doing this Fall. If you expect to be doing two things *simultaneously*, circle both. If you are considering two *alternative* plans, circle only the more probable.

Working full time at a type of job which I expect to be my long run career field 2   (9)
Non-career military service 3   1
Working full time at a civilian job which will probably *not* be my long run career field. 4
Housewife. 5
Graduate study in an arts and science field (physical science, biological science, social science, humanities) 6
Graduate study in a professional field (law, medicine, engineering, education, agriculture, social work, etc.) 7
Other (Circle and specify: _____) 8

2. How definite are the plans you circled in question 1? (Circle one.)

Quite definite x	(10)
Fairly definite, but subject to change 0	Y
Quite indefinite 1	

3. If you are considering a set of alternative plans, different from the ones you circled in question 1, indicate them by circling the appropriate numbers below, using the categories from question 1.

If you have no alternative plans in mind, circle the number nine below. (11)

      2   3   4   5   6   7   8   9   1

4. At the time you entered college, what were your plans for study beyond the bachelor's degree? (Circle one.)

I planned to go into a line of work which requires graduate or professional training x	(12)
I planned to go on for graduate or professional training, but I didn't have a specific field in mind 0	Y
I planned to stop at the bachelor's degree 1	
I didn't have any definite plans 2	

5. Have you applied for admission to any graduate or professional school for the coming year? (Circle one.)

	(13)
*No, and I do *not* expect to go to school next year 4	9
**No, but I do expect to go to school next year 5	IF 4,
***Yes, I applied to one school 6	SKIP
***Yes, I applied to 2 or 3 schools 7	TO
***Yes, I applied to 4 or more schools 8	COL.
	23

*IF "NO, AND DO NOT EXPECT TO GO TO SCHOOL NEXT YEAR": SKIP TO QUESTION 7.

**IF "NO, BUT I DO EXPECT TO GO TO SCHOOL NEXT YEAR": SKIP TO QUESTION 6.

***IF "YES": PLEASE ANSWER a, b, AND c.

a. How many schools accepted you? (Circle one.)

None 0	(14)
One 1	4
More than one 2	

b. How many schools rejected your application? (Circle one.)

None 5	(15)
One 6	9
More than one 7	

c. Have you any applications pending? (Circle one.)

Yes 0   (16)

No 1   Y

6. Did you apply (or were you nominated) for financial support (scholarship, fellowship, assistantship, etc.) for this Fall? (Circle one.)

*No 7   (17)

**Yes 8   9

*IF "NO": Did you not apply because— (Circle any which apply.)

I had no intention of going to school at the time applications were
  due 0   (18)
I wouldn't need any support of this type 1   Y
The amount I could get would have been too little 2
The duties attached would have been unsatisfactory 3
I didn't think I could get any 4
It didn't occur to me to apply 5
Other (Circle and specify: _____) 6

**IF "YES": PLEASE ANSWER a, b, c, AND d.

a. To where did you apply or was your nomination sent? (Circle one or more.)

The school I will (probably) attend 0   (19)
Other school or schools 1   Y
Other source (government, private foundation, etc.) 2

b. Which ones *offered* you aid? (Circle one or more.)

The school I will (probably) attend 4   (20)
Other school or schools 5   9
Other source (government, private foundation, etc.) 6
No offers 7

c. Which of the following do you expect to *receive* next year: (Circle one or more.)

Scholarship for part tuition 1   (21)
Scholarship for full tuition 2   9
Fellowship for tuition plus an amount under $1,000 3
Fellowship for tuition plus $1,000 or more 4
Teaching assistantship 5
Research assistantship 6
No financial support of this type 7
Don't know yet 8

d. From which of the following source or sources do you expect to receive financial aid (scholarship, fellowship, assistantship, etc.)? (Circle one or more.)

No financial aid of this type expected   1   (22)
School I will attend   2   0
Private foundation, philanthropic organization, etc.   3
U.S. Federal government:
  National Defense Act   4
  National Science Foundation . . . . , ...   5
  Public Health Service — National Institutes of Health   6
  Other   7
State or local government (U.S.)   8
Other (Circle and specify: _____)   9

ARE YOU SURE OR FAIRLY SURE THAT YOU WILL BE ATTENDING GRADUATE OR
PROFESSIONAL SCHOOL NEXT YEAR? (ACADEMIC YEAR 1961 – 1962)?   IF YES,

IF "YES": PUT A CHECK IN THIS BOX AND SKIP TO QUESTION 13 ☐   SKIP TO
COLUMN
IF "NO": ANSWER QUESTION 7 THROUGH 12.   32

---

7. If there were no obstacles in terms of finances, grade records, getting admitted, etc., would you *like* to go on for graduate or professional study in the future?
(Circle one.)

Yes   2   (23)
Maybe   3   5
No   4

---

8. Do you expect to go on for graduate or professional school sometime in the
future? (Circle one.)

No   5   (24)
Probably not   6   9
*Probably yes   7
*Yes   8

---

*IF "PROBABLY YES" OR "YES": PLEASE ANSWER a AND b.

a. Do you expect that your future employer will send you or pay for your
future studies? (Do not count savings from your pay or anticipated veteran's
benefits.) (Circle one.)

Yes   0   (25)
No   1   Y

b. When will you start your graduate or professional studies? Make your
single best prediction. (Circle one.)

Academic Year
'62 – '63   0   (26)
'63 – '64   1   Y
'64 – '65   2
'65 – '66 or after   3
No specific date in mind . .   4

9. Do you have a definite job (including military service) lined up after graduation? (Circle one.)

Yes 6   (27)
No, but I intend to be working 7   9
No, I do not intend to be working 8

10. Since you've been in college, have you at any time considered going on for graduate study or considered an occupation which would require professional training beyond a bachelor's degree? (Circle one.)

I never thought of it 2   (28)
I thought about it, but I never considered it seriously 3   1
I considered it seriously, but decided against it 4
I do plan to go on, but not next year 5

---

11. To what extent did immediate financial obstacles (not doubts about the long run economic value of further study) affect your decision regarding graduate or professional school *next year*? (Circle one.)

Financial obstacles had nothing to do with it 6   (29)
*Financial obstacles played some part in my decision 7   9
*Financial obstacles are the major reason I am not going on for
   further study next year 8

* Listed below are some selected types of financial assistance. Circle *any* type which in itself (not in combination with the others) would have made it possible for you to go on to graduate or professional school next year.

Tuition Scholarship 0   (30)
Fellowship for tuition plus $1,000 cash 1   9
Loan for tuition which would not have to be paid back until I was
   out of school 2
Loan for tuition plus living expenses which would not have to be
   paid back until I was out of school 3
10–20 hour a week job as a teaching or research assistant 4
Financial help from my parents 5
Payment of all my current debts for undergraduate education . . . 6
None of these 7

---

12. Which of the following best explains why you do not anticipate going to graduate or professional school next year? (Circle any which apply.)

No desire to do so . . . . y   (31)
Can get a desirable job without further schooling 0   SP
Financial obstacles 1
Low grades in college 2
Family responsibilities 3
I would rather get married 4
I want to get practical experience first 5
I don't think I have the ability 6
I lack the necessary undergraduate course prerequisites 7
I'm tired of being a student 8

Military service 9
I will be in a company training program which provides the equivalent x

SKIP TO QUESTION 18, "FIELDS AND CAREERS"   SKIP TO
                                                     COLUMN
                                                     38

IF YOU ARE SURE OR FAIRLY SURE THAT YOU WILL BE ATTENDING GRADUATE
OR PROFESSIONAL SCHOOL NEXT YEAR, ANSWER QUESTIONS 13–17.

13. Have you decided upon the specific school you will attend? (Circle one.)

Yes 7   (32)
No 8   9

14. Write below the name of the school that you will most probably attend next
Fall.

_____   _____   _____
(Name of School)   (City)   (State or Country)

a. Is the above school the one you are now attending? (Circle one.)

Yes 4   (33)
No 5   6

15. If you were absolutely free to choose (ignoring finances, admissions, etc.)
would you prefer to— (Circle one.)

Go to the same school I expect to attend next year 0   (34)
*Attend a different school 1   Y

*IF "ATTEND A DIFFERENT SCHOOL": Did any of the following prevent you
from attending the school you would really prefer? (Circle any which apply.)

Wasn't offered any financial support (scholarship, fellowship, assist-
antship). 2   (35)
Was offered support, but it was too little 3   9
Was refused admission or didn't apply because I thought I would be
refused 4
Financial obstacles other than scholarship, assistantship, etc. 5
Limited to schools in a particular community 6
Other (Circle and specify: _____) 7

16. If you were absolutely free to choose (ignoring finances, admissions, etc.)
would you prefer to— (Circle one.)

Study in the same field I will be in 0   (36)
*Study in a different field 1   Y

*IF "STUDY IN A DIFFERENT FIELD": Did any of the following prevent you from studying in the field which you really prefer? (Circle any which apply.)

Wasn't offered any financial support (scholarship, fellowship, assistantship)	2	(37)
Was offered support, but it was too little	3	9
Was refused admission or didn't apply because I thought I would be refused	4	
Financial obstacles other than scholarship, assistantship, etc.	5	
Limited to schools in a particular community	6	
Other (Circle and specify: _____)	7	

17. In terms of your finances during the next academic year when you are in graduate or professional school, from which of the following sources do you expect to receive $200 or more? (Circle any which apply.)

Full time job	1	(38)
Part time job other than teaching or research assistantship	2	9
Withdrawals from savings	3	
National Defense Education Act Loan	4	
Other Loan	5	
Parents or relatives	6	
Income from spouse's employment	7	
Other (Circle and specify: _____)	8	

IMPORTANT

The following list of fields is to be used in answering Questions 18 through 24. Read the instructions for these questions found on page 8 before using the list.

Business and Administration
92 Accounting
90 Advertising, Public Relations
9X Military Service, Military Science
97 Secretarial Science (or employed as a secretary)
72 Industrial or Personnel Psychology
91 All other business and commercial fields (Business Administration, Marketing, Insurance, Finance, Industrial Relations, etc.)
93 Public Administration (or employed as government administrator if not covered by other fields)

Engineering
10 Aeronautical
11 Civil (including Agricultural, Architectural, Civil, Sanitary)

12 Chemical (including Ceramic)
13 Electrical
14 Engineering Science, Engineering Physics, Engineering Mechanics
15 Industrial
16 Mechanical (including Naval Architecture and Marine, Welding, Textile)
17 Metallurgical
18 Mining (including Mining, Geological, Geophysical, Petroleum)
1X Engineering, General and other specialties

Physical Science (NOTE: Secondary School Science Teaching is classified under Education)
01 Astronomy, Astrophysics
02 Chemistry (excluding Biochemistry which is 32)

03 Physics (excluding Biophysics which is 34)
04 Geography
05 Geology, Geophysics
06 Oceanography
07 Metallurgy
08 Meteorology (Atmospheric sciences)
0X Physical Science, General and other specialties
09 *Mathematics and Statistics* (NOTE: Secondary School Mathematics Teaching is classified under Education)

Education (NOTE: Junior College, and University Teaching should be coded by Field of Specialization, not as Education)
50 *Elementary* (including Kindergarten and Nursery School)
   Secondary — Academic Subject Fields
51 English
52 Modern Foreign Languages
53 Latin, Greek
54 History, Social Studies
55 Natural Science (General, Physics, Chemistry, Biology, etc.)
56 Mathematics
   Specialized Teaching Fields
57 Physical Education, Health, Recreation
58 Music Education
59 Art Education
60 Education of Exceptional Children (Including Speech Correction)
61 Agricultural Education
62 Home Economics Education
63 Business Education
64 Trade and Industrial Education (Vocational)
65 Industrial Arts Education (Non-Vocational)
66 Counseling and Guidance
67 Educational Psychology
68 Administration and Supervision
6X Education, General and other specialties

Health Professions
20 Dentistry or Pre-Dentistry

21 Medicine or Pre-Medicine
22 Nursing
23 Optometry
24 Pharmacy
25 Physical Therapy
26 Occupational Therapy
27 Veterinary Medicine or Pre-Veterinary
28 Medical Technology or Dental Hygiene
2X Other Health Fields

Biological Sciences
30 Anatomy
31 Biology
32 Biochemistry
33 Botany and Related Plant Sciences (Plant Pathology, Plant Physiology, etc.)
34 Biophysics
35 Entomology
36 Genetics
37 Microbiology (including Bacteriology, Mycology, Parasitology, Virology, etc.)
38 Pathology
39 Pharmacology
40 Physiology
41 Zoology
3X Other Biological Science Fields

Agricultural and Related Fields
45 Agricultural Sciences (including Animal Husbandry, Agronomy, Farm Management, Horticulture, Soil Science, Soil Conservation, etc.)
46 Forestry, Fish and Wild Life Management
27 Veterinary Medicine
47 Farming (Code as occupation only, not as field of study)

Psychology (NOTE: Code Psychiatry as Medicine 21)
70 Clinical Psychology
66 Counseling and Guidance
67 Educational Psychology
71 Social Psychology
72 Industrial and Personnel Psychology

73 Experimental and General Psychology

74 Other Psychological Fields

Social Sciences

75 Anthropology, Archeology

76 Economics

04 Geography

83 History

77 Area and Regional Studies

78 Political Science, Government, International Relations

93 Public Administration

79 Sociology

96 Social Work, Group Work

7X Social Science, General and Other

Humanities

80 Fine and Applied Arts (Art, Music, Speech, Drama, etc.)

81 English, Creative Writing

82 Classical Languages and Literatures

83 History

84 Modern Foreign Languages and Literatures

85 Philosophy

8X Humanities, General and Other Fields

Other Fields and Occupations

86 Architecture, City Planning

94 Foreign Service (Code as occupation only, not field of study)

98 Home Economics (Code either as a field of study or as an occupation if you mean working as a home economist for pay)

99 Housewife (Code as occupation only, not as field of study)

87 Journalism, Radio-Television, Communications

95 Law, Pre-Law

88 Library Science, Archival Science

96 Social Work, Group Work

89 Theology, Religion (Employment as a Clergyman or religious worker)

X0 *Field of Study or Job Which has no Near Equivalent in This List* (If you use this code, please describe your field in a word or two under the questions where it applies.)

X1 *Do not expect to be either employed full time or to be a Housewife* (Code only for questions about careers, not for field of study.)

II. FIELDS AND CAREERS

On pages 6 and 7 of this questionnaire is a list of fields of study and employment. Each one can be used to describe a field of study or a type of job. Thus, for example, in questions about fields of study, "Psychology" means college courses in psychology; in questions about careers, "Psychology" means the occupation of psychologist.

IMPORTANT
NOTE:

When you have chosen the field or occupation from the list which is your answer to one of the questions below, please write the two numbers or letters of that field in the double box at the end of that question. For example, if "Clinical Psychology" is now your major field, write its code number (70) in the boxes at the end of question 18 thus:

⬚⬚

18. Present major field?

If you have a joint major, give the one with the most course credits. ☐☐ (39–40)
x   x

19. Previous major field?

If you have not shifted majors, write "yy" in the boxes.
If you have several previous majors, give the *first* one in which officially registered. ☐☐ (41–42)
x   x

20. Future graduate or professional major?

If you do not plan to ever go to graduate or professional school, write "yy" in the boxes.
If you plan study in several fields, give the *main* one. ☐☐ (43–44)
x   x

21. Anticipated career field?

Please give what you expect to be your long-run career and ignore any school, stop-gap job, or temporary military service which might precede it.

If you are a woman, use "Housewife (99)" only if you do not expect to work full time until your children are grown.

In addition to writing the code in the boxes, please describe your anticipated career in a few words here: _____ ☐☐ (45–46)
x   x

22. Possible alternative career field?

If none, write "yy" in the boxes.
If your alternative has the same code number as the one to question 21, write "yy" in the boxes.
If more than one alternative, give the most likely only. ☐☐ (47–48)
x   x

23. Career preference when you started college?

Give your single strongest preference even if it was vague or or if there were several alternatives.

If absolutely no preference, write "yy" in the boxes. ☐☐ (49–50)
x   x

24. Any alternative career field seriously considered during college which is not mentioned in questions 21, 22, or 23?

If none, write "yy" in the boxes. ☐☐ (51–52)
x   x

NOTE: THE NEXT THREE QUESTIONS REFER TO YOUR ANSWER TO QUESTION 21 (ANTICIPATED CAREER FIELD). IF YOU CODED "99" OR "x1" AS YOUR ANSWER TO QUESTION 21, PLEASE SKIP TO QUESTION 28. OTHERWISE, ANSWER ALL THREE QUESTIONS.

25. Which of the following will be your most likely employer when you begin full time work in your anticipated career field? (If you have a definite expectation, circle one; if not, circle the most likely possibilities.)

Private company with 100 or more employees . . . . Y   (53)
Private company with fewer than 100 employees or professional   SP
   partnership. X
Family business 0
Self-employed 1
Research organization or institute 2
College or University or Junior College 3
Elementary or Secondary School or School System 4
Other educational institutions (e.g. Technical Vocational School) . . 5
Federal Government (U.S.) 6
State or Local Government 7
Hospital, Church, Clinic, Welfare Organization, etc. 8
Other (Circle and specify: _____) 9

26. How do you feel about the occupation which you checked as your anticipated career field? (Circle one.)

I strongly prefer it to any other 0   (54)
I could be tempted by one or more alternatives 1   Y
I would prefer one or more alternatives 2

27. The following activities cut across a number of specific jobs. Which ones do you anticipate will be an important part of your long run career work? (Circle any which apply.)

Teaching 3   (55)
Research 4   9
Administration 5
Service to patients or clients 6
None of these 7

28. Regardless of your career plans now, when you first enrolled as a freshman in college did you have— (Circle one.)

One particular kind of work in mind 5   (56)
Two or more alternative kinds of work in mind 6   9
No specific career plans at that time 7
Planned to be a housewife 8

29. Which of these characteristics would be very important to you in picking a job or career? (Circle as many as apply.)

Making a lot of money . . . . Y   (57)
Opportunities to be original and creative X   SP

Opportunities to be helpful to others or useful to society 0
Avoiding a high pressure job which takes too much out of you . . 1
Living and working in the world of ideas 2
Freedom from supervision in my work 3
Opportunities for moderate but steady progress rather than the
  chance of extreme success or failure 4
A chance to exercise leadership 5
Remaining in the city or area in which I grew up 6
Getting away from the city or area in which I gew up 7
Opportunity to work with people rather than things 8
None of these 9

30. Listed below are six groups of occupations. The occupations within each group are similar to each other in many ways.

In Column A, circle the *two types* you would like best.

In Column B, circle the *two types* you would like least.

Consider the jobs as a group, not particular ones, and rate them only in terms of whether you would like that *type* of work regardless of whether such jobs are realistic career possibilities. Disregard considerations of salary, social standing, future advancement, etc.

Occupations	A. Two Best Liked Groups	B. Two Least Liked Groups	
Construction inspector, electrician, engineer, radio operator, tool designer, weather observer	x	x	
Physicist, anthropologist, astronomer, biologist, botanist, chemist	0	0	(58) (59) Y Y
Social worker, clinical psychologist, employment interviewer, high school teacher, physical education teacher, public relations man .	1	1	
Bank teller, financial analyst, IBM equipment operator, office manager, statistician, tax expert	2	2	
Business executive, buyer, hotel manager, radio program director, real estate salesman, sales engineer	3	3	
Actor, commercial artist, musician, newspaper reporter, stage director, writer	4	4	

31. Please circle all the statements which describe your feelings about these specific occupations. (Circle as many or as few as apply in each column.)

	(60) SP	(61) SP	(62) SP	(63) SP	(64) SP	(65) SP
	Research Physicist or Chemist	College Professor	High School Teacher	Physician	Engineer	Business Executive
his sort of work would be very interesting	Y	Y	Y	Y	Y	Y
don't have the ability to do this kind of work	X	X	X	X	X	X
probably couldn't make as much money at this type of work as I'd like to make	0	0	0	0	0	0
ne would have to devote too much time and energy to this work. I want to be able to spend more time with my family and friends	1	1	1	1	1	1
ne would have to invest more time and money in preparing for this occupation than I feel I could afford	2	2	2	2	2	2
know as a personal friend, or family friend, one or more people in this field	3	3	3	3	3	3
y parents would disapprove of my going into this field.	4	4	4	4	4	4
y personality isn't suitable for work in this field	5	5	5	5	5	5
eople with my religious, racial, or family background don't have much chance of success in this field	6	6	6	6	6	6
ouldn't be challenging enough for me	7	7	7	7	7	7
wouldn't like the life I'd have to lead outside the job	8	8	8	8	8	8
his is my father's occupation . .	9	9	9	9	9	9

32. Please rate the following in terms of their effect on your career plans or decisions during college. (Circle one in each row.)

	Very Important	Fairly Important	Un-important	Never Received Any	
a. Vocational or similar psychological tests	5	6	7	8	(66) 9
b. Discussions with my academic advisor .	0	1	2	3	(67) 4
c. Discussions with faculty members other than my advisor	5	6	7	8	(68) 9
d. Advice from parents	0	1	2	3	(69) 4
e. Interviews with a professional psychological or vocational counselor	5	6	7	8	(70) 9

33. a. What is your opinion about the recently established Peace Corps? (Circle one.)

An excellent program about which I am enthusiastic 2   (71)
A good idea of which I am very much in favor 3   9
A good idea but I am not enthusiastic 4
Probably a good idea but I am not enthusiastic 5
Probably not a good idea but I am not sure 6
Definitely not a good idea 7
Don't know enough about it to have an opinion 8

  b. What are you personally likely to do about the Peace Corps? (Circle one.)

Definitely not volunteer 0   (72)
Am thinking about volunteering but have not made up my mind   Y
  yet 1
Have thought about volunteering but probably would not 2
Am probably going to volunteer 3
Have already volunteered 4
I am not sure what I will do 5

  c. Have you filled out the Peace Corps Questionnaire? (Circle one.)

Yes 6   (73)
No, but I intend to do so . . 7   9
Definitely No 8

  d. Here are some reasons young people have given for their personal reactions to the Peace Corps. Designate reasons both for volunteering and for not volunteering if both kinds seem pertinent to you. (Circle any which apply in your own case.)

  (1) Reasons for volunteering:

To make a personal contribution to world peace 3   (74)
The attraction of working closely with others 4   9
The opportunity to learn about foreign cultures and languages . . 5
It would give me a chance to decide what kind of career I really
  want 6
To help the poorer nations of the world improve their economic
  conditions 7
It would further my career 8

  (2) Reasons for *not* volunteering:

Family and personal obligations 1   (75)
Not eligible on physical grounds 2   9
Opposed to the general idea of a Peace Corps 3
It would interrupt my career 4
Too long a period of service 5
Low pay, undesirable working conditions, etc. 6
I don't have skills which would be useful to the Peace Corps . . . 7
My personality isn't suitable for that type of service 8

III. COLLEGE EXPERIENCE

34. Did you do all of your college work at this school? (Circle one.)

Yes	x	(9)
No, transferred after freshman year	0	Y
No, transferred after sophomore year	1	
No, transferred after junior year	2	
No, started here, attended a year or more elsewhere, and then returned	3	

35. Were you regularly employed during this academic year? (Circle any which apply.)

No	4	(10)
Yes—		9
Full time job which is relevant to my anticipated career field . . .	5	
Full time job which has nothing to do with my anticipated career field	6	
Part time job which is relevant to my anticipated career field . . .	7	
Part time job which has nothing to do with my anticipated career field	8	

36. In which of the following have you been an active participant at this school? (Circle any which apply.)

Editorial staff of campus publication	0	(11)
Musical or dramatic group	1	Y
Business staff of campus publication or other campus group . . .	2	
Campus group concerned with national or world issues	3	
Inter-collegiate (varsity) athletics	4	
Fraternity, Sorority (or equivalent)	5	
Special interest group (e.g., Psychology Club, Outing Club)	6	
Student government	7	
Other (Circle and specify: _____)	8	
None	9	

37. Please call to mind the students of your own sex who are your closest friends here. Where did you meet them? (Circle any which apply)

Knew them before I came here	x	(12)
Dormitory or rooming house	0	Y
My Fraternity or Sorority (or equivalent)	1	
Campus activities	2	
Classes in my major field	3	
Classes in other fields	4	
Other (Circle and specify:_____)	5	
No close friends here	6	

38. Of your close friends here, how many are going on next year for graduate or professional studies? (Circle one.)

All or almost all . . . . x (13)
More than half . . . . 0 Y
Less than half 1
Few or none 2
No close friends here 3

39. Which of the following best describes where you lived this year? (Circle any which apply.)

Fraternity, Sorority (or equivalent) 5 (14)
Dormitory or other campus housing 6 9
Off-Campus room, apartment, house 7
With my parents 8

40. Listed below are some college courses which you might have taken. Please circle the number of any statements which describe your reactions. (Circle any which apply in each row. If none apply, leave the row blank.)

	(15) 9	(16) 9	(17) 9	(18) 9	(19) 9

Course or Area

	Physics, Chemistry	Mathe- matics	Biology, Zoology, Botany	Social Sciences	English
I took one or more courses in this field or area during college	x	x	x	x	x
I *didn't* take any courses in this field or area during college	0	0	0	0	0
I found this course content very interesting . . .	1	1	1	1	1
I found this course content very dull	2	2	2	2	2
I have a flair for course work in this area	3	3	3	3	3
I found this area rough going academically . . .	4	4	4	4	4
Teachers in this area encouraged me to go on in the field	5	5	5	5	5
I admire many of the teachers in this area as persons not just as professors	6	6	6	6	6
By and large, the teachers in this area are *not* the kind of person I'd like to be	7	7	7	7	7
One or more of my close friends is majoring in this	8	8	8	8	8

41. Listed below are some purposes or results of college. Circle the one which is most important to you personally, and also circle the one which you think is most important to the typical student here. (Circle one in each column.)

	Most Important to me Personally	Most Important to the Typical Student here	
A basic general education and appreciation of ideas	0	5	
Having a good time while getting a degree	1	6	(20) (21)
Career training	2	7	4 9
Developing the ability to get along with different kinds of people	3	8	

42. Have you had any experience in original research (participating in collecting and analyzing raw data or conducting an experiment, *not* writing papers based on published sources or doing experiments from a laboratory manual) during your college studies? (Circle any which apply.)

No, I have never participated in original research 2   (22)
Yes, I have —   9

  a. Participated in research as part of a course 3
  b. Been employed by a faculty member as a research assistant   4
  c. Had an off-campus job (summer or during school year) working
     in research 5
  d. Participated in a summer research training program sponsored
     by the government or private foundation 6
  e. Conducted a research project on my own (e.g. senior thesis)   7
  f. Other (Circle and specify:_____)   8

43. What is your current academic status? (Circle one.)

Registered Spring term and studying for a bachelor's degree to be
    awarded at Spring commencement (May, June, July, but before
    Summer session commencement) 0   (23)
Registered Spring term and studying for a bachelor's degree to be   3
    awarded at Summer session commencement 1
Other (Circle and briefly specify your academic status: _____
_____) 2

44. When you graduate, how much personal indebtedness will you have for your education? (Count only money you owe for tuition or living costs during school not payments on car, appliances, clothes, etc.) (Circle one.)

              None 5   (24)
              Some, but less than $500 . . 6   9
              $500–$999 7
              $1,000 or more 8

45. What is your overall (cumulative) grade point average for undergraduate work at your present college?

IMPORTANT: If your school uses letter grades (A, B, C, etc.) please circle the code number which is closest to your letter grade average.

Warning: The number which you circle probably does not correspond to the number equivalent at your school, e.g. at most schools "straight A" equals 4.0, here it equals "0".

If your school does not use letter grades, there should be special instructions accompanying your questionnaire. If, through clerical error, the instructions are missing, write your average in the margin.

(Circle one.)

	Letter Grade	Code Number	
	A	0	(25)
	A−	1	Y
	B+	2	
	B	3	
	B−	4	
	C+	5	
	C	6	
	C−	7	
	D+	8	
	D or lower	9	

46. Listed below are a number of awards and honors. Which of these have you received during college or which are you fairly sure you will receive by the time you graduate? (Circle any which apply.)

Dean's List	Y	(26)
Phi Beta Kappa	X	SP
Other honor society based on academic achievement	0	
Graduation with honors (cum) (Magna) (Summa)	1	
National Merit Scholarship holder, Finalist, or Semi-Finalist . . .	2	
Other scholarship awarded on basis of academic ability	3	
Participation in "honors program" at this school	4	
Prize or award for scholarship or research work (e.g. "Smith prize for best biology experiment")	5	
Prize or award for literary, musical, or artistic work	6	
Took one or more graduate level courses as an undergraduate . .	7	
Other award or honor	8	
No special honors	9	

47. As best you know, how do you stand among the other people graduating in the *same major field* at your school? (Circle one.)

Top 10 per cent	4	(27)
Top quarter, but not top 10 per cent	5	9
Second quarter	6	
Third quarter	7	
Lowest quarter	8	

48. What is your emotional feeling about your college or university? (Circle one.)

I have a very strong attachment to it	x	(28)
I like it, but my feelings are not strong	0	Y
Mixed feelings	1	
I don't like it much, but my feelings are not strong	2	
I thoroughly dislike it	3	

IV. PERSONAL CHARACTERISTICS

49. Your age at your last birthday? (Circle one.)

19 or younger	0	(29)
20	1	Y
21	2	
22	3	
23 – 24	4	
25 – 29	5	
30 or older	6	

50. Sex. (Circle one.)

Male	7	(30)
Female	8	9

51. Marital Status. (Circle one.)

Single, don't expect to be married before Fall, 1961	4	(31)
*Single, expect to be married before Fall, 1961	5	9
*Married, one or more children or expecting a child	6	
*Married, no children	7	
Widowed, Divorced, Separated	8	

*IF "MARRIED" OR "EXPECTING TO BE MARRIED BEFORE FALL, 1961": What will your spouse or future spouse most likely be doing next year? (Circle any which apply.)

Working full time	3	(32)
Working part time	4	9
Housewife, Mother	5	
Going to School	6	
Military Service	7	

52. Religion:

a. In which you were reared. (Circle one.)

Protestant (Circle and specify) _____	x	(33)
Roman Catholic	0	Y
Jewish	1	
Other (Circle and specify: _____)	2	
None	3	

b. Your present preference. (Circle one.)

Protestant (Circle and specify: _____) 5 (34)
Roman Catholic 6   4
Jewish 7
Other (Circle and specify: _____) 8
None 9

---

53. Your racial background. (Circle one.)

White . . . . x (35)
Negro 0   Y
Oriental 1
Other (Circle and specify: _____) 2

---

54. How many—

a. *Older* brothers or sisters do you have? (Circle one.)

None 0 (36)
One 1   4
Two 2
Three or more 3

---

b. *Younger* brothers or sisters do you have? (Circle one.)

None 5 (37)
One 6   9
Two 7
Three or more 8

---

55. Are you a U.S. citizen? (Circle one.)

Yes, U.S. born . . . . x (38)
Yes, Naturalized 0   Y
No, but I expect to stay in the U.S. 1
No, and I do not expect to stay in the U.S. 2

---

56. Please indicate your parents' (or step-parent's if parent is dead) highest educational attainment. (Circle one in each column.)

	Father	Mother	
8th grade or less	3	3	(39) (40)
Part High School	4	4	9 9
High School graduate	5	5	
Part College	6	6	
College graduate	7	7	
Graduate or professional degree beyond the bachelor's	8	8	

57 a. Which of the following categories best describes the usual occupation of the head of the household in your parental family? (Circle one.)

Professional 1   (41)
Proprietor or Manager 2   Y
Sales (Other than Sales Manager or Administrator) 3
Clerical 4
Skilled worker 5
Semi-Skilled worker 6
Service worker 7
Unskilled worker 8
Farmer or farm worker 9

   b. If the head of the household is a woman, also circle here 0
   c. If the head of the household is retired, also circle here x

58. Which of the following is the appropriate income category for your parental family? Consider annual income from all sources before taxes. (Circle one.)

Less than $5,000 per year . . 2   (42)
$5,000 – $7,499 3   9
$7,500 – $9,999 4
$10,000 – $14,999 5
$15,000 – $19,999 6
$20,000 and over 7
I have no idea 8

59. Which of the following best describes the community which you think of as your home town during high school days? (Circle one.)

Farm or open country x   (43)
                                                Y
Suburb in a metropolitan area of—

more than 2 million population 0
500,000 to 2 million 1
100,000 to 499,999 2
less than 100,000 3

Central city in a metropolitan area or city of—

more than 2 million population 4
500,000 to 2 million 5
100,000 to 499,999 6
50,000 to 99,999 7
10,000 to 49,999 8
less than 10,000 9

60. Which of the following best describes the distance between your home town (when you were in high school) and your current college? (Circle one.)

In the same city or within commuting distance x   (44)
Within four hours automobile drive or less 0   Y

More than four hours drive, but in the same state 1
More than four hours drive, but in a different state 2

61. Please rate yourself on the following dimensions as you really think you are. (Circle one in each row.)

	Very	Fairly	Neither	Fairly	Very		
a. Unfavorable toward modern art	Y	x	0	1	2	Favorable toward modern art	(45) 3
b. Politically liberal	4	5	6	7	8	Politically conservative	(46) 9
c. Conventional in opinions and values	Y	x	0	1	2	Unconventional in opinions and values	(47) 3
d. Religious	4	5	6	7	8	Non-religious	(48) 9

62. Listed below are some adjectives, some of which are "favorable," some of which are "unfavorable," some of which are neither.

Please circle the ones which best describe you. Consider only those which are most characteristic of you as a person. (Most people choose five or six, but you may choose more or fewer if you want to.)

(49) SP	(50) SP	(51) SP
Ambitious x	Good Looking x	Moody x
Athletic 0	Happy 0	Obliging 0
Calm 1	Hard Driving 1	Outgoing 1
Cautious 2	High Strung 2	Poised 2
Cooperative 3	Idealistic 3	Quiet 3
Cultured 4	Impetuous 4	Rebellious 4
Dominant 5	Intellectual 5	Reserved 5
Easy Going 6	Lazy 6	Shy 6
Energetic 7	Low Brow 7	Sophisticated 7
Forceful 8	Methodical 8	Talkative 8
Fun Loving 9	Middle Brow 9	Witty 9

Appendix 2

Spring, 1962 Questionnaire College Graduate Survey

NATIONAL OPINION RESEARCH CENTER

University of Chicago
5720 Woodlawn Avenue, Chicago 37, Illinois

Dear 1961 Graduate: May, 1962

Last spring you filled out a questionnaire about your plans for post-graduate work and study.

We are coming back to you again with the attached questionnaire to find out what you are doing this year and what are your plans for the future.

Thirty-four thousand seniors from 135 colleges and universities filled out questionnaires last spring. We are hoping for the same excellent cooperation this year.

Your reply is essential to construct an accurate account of what happened to last year's graduates. Please fill out the questionnaire whether you are working or not working, going to school or not going to school.

This research is being supported by federal agencies and private foundations concerned with manpower and higher education.

When we receive your completed questionnaire, we will mail to you a summary of the major findings from last year's survey.

Thank you for your cooperation.

Sincerely,

James A. Davis
Senior Study Director

P.S. The inside pages of this cover letter contain instructions for filling out the questionnaire.

FIELD LIST

The following field list is to be used in answering some or all of the following questions: 11, 18, 19, 30A, B, and C, 44B, 47D, 48A. Each field can be used to describe a field of study or a type of job. Thus, for example, in questions about fields of study, "psychology" means college courses in psychology; in questions about careers, "psychology" means the occupation of psychologist.

When you have chosen from the list the field or occupation which is your answer to a given question, please write the two numbers or letters of that field in the double box at the end of the question. For example, if "clinical psychology" is the answer to the question asked, write its code number (70) in the boxes provided, such as: $\boxed{7}\boxed{0}$

Business and Administration

92 Accounting
90 Advertising, Public Relations
9X Military Service, Military Science
97 Secretarial Science (or employed as a secretary)
72 Industrial or Personnel Psychology
91 All other business and commercial fields (Business Administration, Marketing, Insurance, Finance, Industrial Relations, etc.)
93 Public Administration (or employed as government administrator if not covered by other fields)

12 Chemical (including Ceramic)
13 Electrical
14 Engineering Science, Engineering Physics, Engineering Mechanics
15 Industrial
16 Mechanical (including Naval Architecture and Marine, Welding, Textile)
17 Metallurgical
18 Mining (including Mining, Geological, Geophysical, Petroleum)
1X Engineering, General and other specialties

Physical Science (NOTE: Secondary School Science Teaching is classified under Education)

Engineering
10 Aeronautical
11 Civil (including Agricultural, Architectural, Civil, Sanitary)
03 Physics (excluding Biophysics which is 34)
04 Geography
05 Geology, Geophysics
06 Oceanography
07 Metallurgy
08 Meteorology (Atmospheric sciences)
0X Physical Science, General and other specialties
09 *Mathematics and Statistics* (NOTE: Secondary School Mathematics Teaching is classified under Education)

Education (NOTE: Junior College, and University Teaching should be coded by Field of Specialization, not as Education)
50 *Elementary* (including Kindergarten and Nursery School)
   Secondary — Academic Subject Fields
51 English
52 Modern Foreign Languages
53 Latin, Greek
54 History, Social Studies
55 Natural Science (General, Physics, Chemistry, Biology, etc.)
56 Mathematics
   Specialized Teaching Fields
57 Physical Education, Health, Recreation
58 Music Education
59 Art Education
60 Education of Exceptional Children (Including Speech Correction)
61 Agricultural Education
62 Home Economics Education
63 Business Education
64 Trade and Industrial Education (Vocational)
65 Industrial Arts Education (Non-Vocational)
66 Counseling and Guidance
67 Educational Psychology

01 Astronomy, Astrophysics
02 Chemistry (excluding Biochemistry which is 32)
21 Medicine or Pre-Medicine
22 Nursing
23 Optometry
24 Pharmacy
25 Physical Therapy
26 Occupational Therapy
27 Veterinary Medicine or Pre-Veterinary
28 Medical Technology or Dental Hygiene
2X Other Health Fields

Biological Sciences
30 Anatomy
31 Biology
32 Biochemistry
33 Botany and Related Plant Sciences (Plant Pathology, Plant Physiology, etc.)
34 Biophysics
35 Entomology
36 Genetics
37 Microbiology (including Bacteriology, Mycology, Parasitology, Virology, etc.)
38 Pathology
39 Pharmacology
40 Physiology
41 Zoology
3X Other Biological Science Fields

Agricultural and Related Fields
45 Agricultural Sciences (including Animal Husbandry, Agronomy, Farm Management, Horticulture, Soil Science, Soil Conservation, etc.)
46 Forestry, Fish and Wild Life Management
27 Veterinary Medicine
47 Farming (Code as occupation only, not as field of study)

Psychology (NOTE: Code Psychiatry as Medicine 21)

68 Administration and Supervision
6X Education, General and other specialties

Health Professions
20 Dentistry or Pre-Dentistry
73 Experimental and General Psychology
74 Other Psychological Fields

Social Sciences
75 Anthropology, Archeology
76 Economics
04 Geography
83 History
77 Area and Regional Studies
78 Political Science, Government, International Relations
93 Public Administration
79 Sociology
96 Social Work, Group Work
7X Social Science, General and Other

Humanities
80 Fine and Applied Arts (Art, Music, Speech, Drama, etc.)
81 English, Creative Writing
82 Classical Languages and Literatures
83 History
84 Modern Foreign Languages and Literatures
85 Philosophy
8X Humanities, General and Other Fields

70 Clinical Psychology
66 Counseling and Guidance
67 Educational Psychology
71 Social Psychology
72 Industrial and Personnel Psychology

Other Fields and Occupations
86 Architecture, City Planning
94 Foreign Service (Code as occupation only, not field of study)
98 Home Economics (Code either as a field of study or as an occupation if you mean working as a home economist for pay)
99 Housewife (Code as occupation only, not as field of study)
87 Journalism, Radio-Television, Communications
95 Law, Pre-Law
88 Library Science, Archival Science
96 Social Work, Group Work
89 Theology, Religion (Employment as a Clergyman or religious worker)

X0 *Field of Study or Job Which has no Near Equivalent in This List* (If you use this code, please describe your field in a word or two under the questions where it applies.)

X1 *Do not expect to be either employed full time or to be a Housewife* (Code only for questions about careers, not for field of study.)

INSTRUCTIONS

The questionnaire requires 30 minutes or so to fill out. Please answer the questions as frankly and accurately as you can. Your answers will be absolutely confidential, and no individual student's answers will be revealed in the reports, which will be based on statistical tabulations.

Almost all of the questions can be answered by drawing a circle around one or more numbers or letters in the right hand margins of the questionnaire. Thus:

What are you doing this spring? (CIRCLE ANY WHICH APPLY)

Working full time 4
Working part time . . .(5)
Military service (full-
time active duty) . . . 6
Housewife, mother . . . 7
Going to school . . . . .(8)
Other (CIRCLE AND
SPECIFY) _____ 9

NOTE: After each question there are instructions in parentheses. Please follow these instructions closely as they are very important for data processing.

A. If it says "(CIRCLE ONE)," draw a circle around only the one number or letter which *best describes* your answer, even though one or more other alternatives might be relevant.
B. If it says "(CIRCLE ONE IN EACH COLUMN)," please look to see that you have circled one and only one number or letter in each of the appropriate columns.
C. If it says "(CIRCLE AS MANY AS APPLY)," circle as many or as few numbers or letters in the columns as you think are relevant.

STIPENDS

Questions 38, 40, and 47 refer to source and types of stipends. This includes any scholarship, fellowship, assistantship, or other stipend.

Exclude loans and gifts from parents.
Include reduction in fees even if the money is not received directly.
Consider work as an assistantship if you are receiving income from teaching or research in your field of study and are paid by your school or an affiliated organization.

FOR EXAMPLE: If you are planning to have a teaching assistantship from your school, write the code number (39) in the boxes provided, such as: 3 9

Lawyers in the Making

Source of Stipend	Type of Stipend				
	Scholarship Equal To or Less Than My Tuition Bill	Scholarship or Fellow-ship for Tuition Plus Cash Grant	Assistantship		Other Stipend Awarded to Students (e.g., Board and Room for Counselors Living in a Dorm)
			Teach-ing	Re-search	
Private foundation, philan-thropic organization, etc.	10	20	30	40	50
U.S. federal government National Defense Educa-tion Act	11	21	31	41	51
National Science Founda-tion	12	22	32	42	52
Public Health Service – National Institutes of Health	13	23	33	43	53
Department of Defense	14	24	34	44	54
Atomic Energy Com-mission	15	25	35	45	55
National Aeronautics and Space Administration	16	26	36	46	56
Other federal government	17	27	37	47	57
State or local government (U.S.)	18	28	38	48	58
My school	19	29	39	49	59
Other (CIRCLE AND SPECIFY)	1x	2x	3x	4x	5x

NATIONAL OPINION RESEARCH CENTER

Survey No. 450
College Graduate Survey
Spring, 1962

BACKGROUND INFORMATION

1. What are you doing this spring? (CIRCLE ANY WHICH APPLY)

Working full time . . . . 4 $\frac{11}{3}$

Working part time . . . 5

Military service (full-time active duty) . . . 6

Housewife, mother . . . 7

Going to school 8

Other (CIRCLE AND SPECIFY) _____ 9

2. What is your current marital status? (CIRCLE ONE)

Single, no definite plans to be married at present . . . . . x $\frac{12}{Y}$

Single, have definite plans to be married *before* Sept. 1, 1962 0

Single, have definite plans to be married, *after* Sept. 1, 1962 1

Widowed, divorced, separated (ANSWER A ONLY) 2

Married (ANSWER A AND B) 3

IF WIDOWED, DIVORCED, SEPARATED, ANSWER A ONLY.
IF MARRIED, ANSWER A AND B.

A. How many children do you have now (count a current pregnancy as one child)? (CIRCLE ONE)

None . . . . 5 $\frac{13}{R}$
One 6
Two 7
Three 8
Four or more 9

B. What is your spouse doing this spring? (CIRCLE ANY WHICH APPLY)

Working full time . . . . x $\frac{14}{R}$
Working part time 0
Military service (full-
    time active duty) . . . 1
Housewife, mother . . . 2
Going to school 3
Other (CIRCLE AND
    SPECIFY) _____ 4

---

3. What is your sex?

Female . . . . 1 $\frac{15}{0}$
Male 2

A. IF FEMALE:
In the long run which one of the following do you prefer and which one do you realistically expect?

	Really Prefer (CIRCLE ONE)	Realistically Expect (CIRCLE ONE)
Housewife only	5	5

Housewife with occasional employment	6	6
Housewife now, employment later	7	7
Combining housewife with employment	8	8
Employment only	9	9
	16	17
	R	R

B. IF MALE:

1) Are you now on full-time active duty in the armed services? (CIRCLE ONE)

Yes (SKIP TO C BELOW) . 0   18
No 1   R

2) IF NO: Have you ever been on full-time active duty in the armed services for a period of at least six months? (CIRCLE ONE)

Yes (SKIP TO C BELOW) . 3   19
No 4   R

3) IF NO: Do you expect to be on active duty in the armed forces for a period of at least six months during the next five or six years? (CIRCLE ONE)

Definitely yes 6   20
Probably yes 7   R
Probably no 8
Definitely no 9

C. How has your military status affected your plans for further education? (CIRCLE AS MANY AS APPLY)

Not at all 5   21
An influence toward: R
postponing entry into
my graduate studies . 6
beginning my graduate
studies sooner 7
interrupting my graduate studies 8
not hurrying through
my graduate studies . 9

4. A. Where are you living now? (CIRCLE ONE)

Farm or open country . . . . x $\frac{22}{Y}$
Suburb in a metropolitan area of
  More than 2 million population 0
  500,000 to 2 million 1
  100,000 to 499,999 2
  Less than 100,000 3
Central city in a metropolitan area of (or non-suburban
  city of)
  More than 2 million population 4
  500,000 to 2 million 5
  100,000 to 499,999 6
  50,000 to 99,999 7
  10,000 to 49,999 8
  Less than 10,000 9

  B. Is the community in which you are now living the one which
    was your home town when you were in high school? (CIRCLE
    ONE)

                Yes . . . . x $\frac{23}{Y}$
                No 0

5. Where were you living when you were in high school and where
do you live now? (CIRCLE ONE IN EACH COLUMN)

Region	State	Hometown during High School (Circle One)	Now Living (Circle One)
New England	Conn., Maine, Mass., N.H., R.I., Vt.	x	x
Middle Atlantic	Del., D.C., Md., N.J., N.Y., Pa.	0	0
East North Central	Ill., Ind., Mich., Ohio, Wis.	1	1
West North Central	Iowa, Kans., Minn., Mo., Nebr., N.D., S.D.	2	2
South	Ala., Fla., Ga., Ky., Miss., N.C., S.C., Tenn., Va., W. Va.	3	3
South Central	Ark., La., Okla., Texas	4	4
Mountain	Ariz., Colo., Idaho, Mont., Nev. N. Mex., Utah, Wyo.	5	5
West	Calif., Oregon, Wash.	6	6
Alaska or Hawaii		7	7
Canada		8	8
Other Non-U.S. (SPECIFY)		9	9
		$\frac{24}{Y}$	$\frac{25}{Y}$

6. Please Indicate:	The Highest Degree You Now Hold (Circle One)	The Next Degree You Expect to Receive (Circle One)	The Highest Degree You Expect to Gain Eventually (Circle One)
None or no further degree	5	x	5
Bachelor's (undergraduate) e.g., B.A., B.S., B.E., B. Phar., etc.	6	0	6
P o s t B a c h e l o r ' s Professional e.g., LL.B., MSW, M.D., J.D., M.Ed., etc.	7	1	7
Arts and Science Master's e.g., M.A., M.S., etc.	8	2	8
Doctorate e.g., Ph.D., Ed.D., J.S.D., etc.	9	3	9
	$\frac{26}{4}$	$\frac{27}{Y}$	$\frac{28}{4}$

7. When did you receive your bachelor's degree? (CIRCLE ONE)

I do not yet have a bachelor's degree . . . . x $\frac{29}{Y}$
Spring commencement, 1961 0
Summer session commencement, 1961 1
Other (SPECIFY) 2

EMPLOYMENT

8. Are you employed now? (Include active military service but not reserve programs.) (CIRCLE ONE)

No . . . . 7 $\frac{30}{6}$
Yes, full time 8
Yes, part time 9

9. Have you worked at any full-time job since last June which you no longer hold? (CIRCLE ONE)

Yes, summer only . . . 2 $\frac{31}{1}$
Yes, other 3
No 4

10. How difficult was it to get a desirable civilian job? (CIRCLE AS MANY AS APPLY)

I don't know because I didn't actually try to get a civilian job x

I continued with job I held before graduation 0

I got the kind of employment I wanted with very little effort 1

I had to look around quite a bit, but I finally got the kind of job I wanted 2

I couldn't find the kind of job I wanted but I didn't look very hard 3

I couldn't find the kind of job I wanted even though I looked very hard 4

$$\frac{32}{Y}$$

IF YOU ARE EMPLOYED NOW, FULL TIME OR PART TIME, ON A CIVILIAN OR MILITARY JOB, ANSWER QUESTIONS 11 THROUGH 17 IN TERMS OF THIS JOB.

IF YOU ARE NOT EMPLOYED NOW, ANSWER QUESTIONS 11 THROUGH 17 IN TERMS OF YOUR MOST RECENT FULL-TIME OR PART-TIME CIVILIAN OR MILITARY JOB.

IF YOU HAVE NOT BEEN EMPLOYED AT ALL SINCE JUNE, 1961, SKIP TO QUESTION 18.

---

11. What field best describes your job? (Inside the letter enclosed with the questionnaire is a list of fields of employment and study [see Field List, pp. 138–40]. ENTER THE CODE NUMBER THAT BEST DESCRIBES YOUR JOB.)   ☐☐ $\dfrac{33-34}{X \quad X}$

---

12. Which of the following best describes your employer? (CIRCLE ANY THAT APPLY)

I am self-employed, or in business owned by my family . Y

Private company with 100 or more employees x

Private company with fewer than 100 employees 0

Professional partnership 1

Research organization or institute 2

College or university or junior college 3

Elementary or secondary school or school system 4

Hospital or clinic 5

Church, welfare, or other non-profit organization 6

Federal government (U.S.) 7

State or local government 8

Other (CIRCLE AND SPECIFY) _____ 9

$$\frac{35}{R}$$

13. Please describe:

    A. What kind of work do you do (e.g., high-school physics teacher, assistant sales engineer, wheat farmer, clothing buyer for department store)? _____

    _____

    B. The two major duties: (1) _____
    (2) _____

14. Whether or not they are important to you, personally, please rate your job in terms of (rate each opportunity as either excellent, average, or poor).

Opportunity (Circle One Each)	Chances for This in My Job			
	Excellent	Average	Poor	
Making a lot of money	x	0	1	$\frac{36}{Y}$
Being original and creative	3	4	5	$\frac{37}{2}$
Being help to others or useful to society	7	8	9	$\frac{38}{6}$
Avoiding a high pressure job which takes too much out of you	x	0	1	$\frac{39}{Y}$
Living and working in the world of ideas	3	4	5	$\frac{40}{2}$
Freedom from supervision in my work	7	8	9	$\frac{41}{6}$
Opportunities for moderate but steady progress rather than the chance of extreme success or failure	x	0	1	$\frac{42}{Y}$
A chance to exercise leadership	3	4	5	$\frac{43}{2}$
Working with people rather than things	7	8	9	$\frac{44}{6}$
Opportunities for advancement	x	0	1	$\frac{45}{Y}$

15. Which of the following describes your employer's policy regarding graduate or professional study for people in your type of job? (CIRCLE ANY WHICH APPLY)

There is no reason for graduate or professional study for people in my type of job, so there is no policy . . . . . x $\quad\frac{46}{Y}$

In-service training provides the equivalent of graduate study 0

Advanced study is officially or unofficially discouraged . 1

Advanced graduate or professional training is useful, but
my employer neither encourages nor discourages it . . 2
Employer encourages advanced study, but does not offer
financial aid 3
Employer would pay (is paying) tuition costs or part of
them 4
Employer would pay (is paying) part salary during advanced study 5
Employer would pay (is paying) full salary and tuition
during advanced graduate or professional training . . . 6

16. How do you feel about your job?

Aspect of Job	Extremely Satisfied	Somewhat Satisfied	Neutral	Somewhat Dissatisfied	Extremely Dissatisfied	
Type of work (CIRCLE ONE)	5	6	7	8	9	$\frac{47}{4}$
Salary (CIRCLE ONE)	5	6	7	8	9	$\frac{48}{4}$
Employer or firm (CIRCLE ONE)	5	6	7	8	9	$\frac{49}{4}$

17. Thinking ahead one year from now, which job situation would you prefer and which job situation do you realistically expect? (CIRCLE ONE IN EACH COLUMN)

Situation	I Would Prefer (Circle One)	I Realistically Expect (Circle One)
Same field of work, same employer	x	5
Same field, different employer	0	6
Different field of work, same employer	1	7
Different field of work, different employer	2	8
Not working full time	3	9
	$\frac{50}{Y}$	$\frac{51}{4}$

CAREER PLANS

EVERYONE PLEASE ANSWER:

18. Which field from the list in cover letter [Appendix 1, pp. 121–23] best describes your anticipated long-run career field? Please give what you expect to be your long-run career and ignore any stop-gap job or temporary military service which might precede it.

> IF YOU ARE A WOMAN: If you plan to combine marriage and work, code the field of employment, not housewife. Use the code number for "housewife" only if you do not expect to work at all. 52–53 □□ X X
>
> In addition to writing the code in the boxes, please describe your anticipated career in a few words here.

---

19. If you were free to choose any field from the list, ignoring obstacles such as finances, time for training, admission requirements, etc., would you still choose the field just listed?

> Yes, I would prefer the same field (WRITE "YY" IN THE BOXES).
>
> No, another field would be preferred (PLEASE INDICATE THE FIELD). 54–55 □□ X X

---

20. Which of these characteristics would be very important to you in picking a job or career? (CIRCLE AS MANY AS APPLY)

Making a lot of money x   56
Opportunities to be original and creative 0   Y
Opportunities to be helpful to others or useful to
  society 1
Avoiding a high pressure job which takes too much out
  of you 2
Living and working in the world of ideas 3
Freedom from supervision in my work 4
Opportunities for moderate but steady progress rather
  than the chance of extreme success or failure 5
A chance to exercise leadership 6
Opportunity to work with people rather than things . . . 7
None of the above 8

21. Which of the following do you expect as your long-run future employer? (IF YOU HAVE A DEFINITE EXPECTATION, CIRCLE ONE; IF NOT, CIRCLE THE MOST LIKELY POSSIBILITIES.)

I plan to be self-employed, or in business owned by my family . . . . Y		57
Private company with 100 or more employees X		R
Private company with fewer than 100 employees 0		
Professional partnership 1		
Research organization or institute 2		
College or university or junior college 3		
Elementary or secondary school or school system 4		
Hospital or clinic 5		
Church, welfare, or other non-profit organization 6		
Federal government (U.S.) 7		
State or local government 8		
Other (CIRCLE AND SPECIFY) _____ 9		
Do not expect employment . . . . R		

22. The following activities cut across a number of specific jobs. Which ones do you anticipate will be an important part of your long-run career work? (CIRCLE ANY WHICH APPLY)

Teaching x		58
Research 0		Y
Administration 1		
Service to patients or clients 2		
None of these 3		

23. Please indicate your parents' (or step-parent's, if parent is dead) highest educational attainment. (CIRCLE ONE IN EACH COLUMN)

Educational Attainment	Father	Mother
Eighth grade or less	4	4
Part high school	5	5
High-school graduate	6	6
Part college	7	7
College graduate	8	8
Graduate or professional degree beyond the bachelor's	9	9
	$\frac{59}{3}$	$\frac{60}{3}$

24. What kind of work did your father do when you were age 16? (IF DECEASED OR RETIRED, GIVE HIS MAJOR OCCUPATION WHEN HE WAS WORKING.)

Occupation _____

Duties _____

25. Have any of your relatives ever worked in the following occupations? (REPORT OCCUPATION EVEN IF THE RELATIVE IS RETIRED OR NO LONGER LIVING. CIRCLE ONE OR MORE ANSWERS IN EACH COLUMN.)

	$\frac{61}{R}$	$\frac{63}{R}$	$\frac{65}{R}$	$\frac{67}{R}$
Occupation	Parents (Circle One or More Numbers in This Column)	Brothers, Sisters (Circle One or More Numbers in This Column)	Grandparents, Great Grandparents (Circle One or More Numbers in This Column)	Uncles, Aunts, Cousins (Circle One or More Numbers in This Column)
No one in this relationship to me or don't know their occupations	x	x	x	x
Civil service employee	0	0	0	0
Elected or appointed public official	1	1	1	1
Foreign service officer	2	2	2	2
Career military officer	3	3	3	3
High-school or grade-school teacher	4	4	4	4
College professor	5	5	5	5
Scientist (other than college professor)	6	6	6	6
Engineer	7	7	7	7
Writer, artist, musician	8	8	8	8
Farmer	9	9	9	9
Blue-collar worker	x	x	x	x
Small business proprietor	0	0	0	0
Executive in a large business	1	1	1	1
Certified public accountant	2	2	2	2
Lawyer	3	3	3	3
Clergyman	4	4	4	4
Physician	5	5	5	5
Other health profession (dentist, pharmacist, nurse, etc.)	6	6	6	6
Social worker	7	7	7	7
Architect	8	8	8	8
None of these occupations	9	9	9	9
	$\frac{62}{R}$	$\frac{64}{R}$	$\frac{66}{R}$	$\frac{68}{R}$

26. Have you enrolled for one or more courses in a program leading to a degree since you were graduated from college? (CIRCLE ONE)

Yes (ANSWER QUESTIONS 27–43) x   11
No (SKIP TO Q. 44). 0   Y

NOTE: FILL OUT QUESTIONS 27–43 IF YOU HAVE ENROLLED THIS ACADEMIC YEAR (1961–62) FOR COURSES APPLICABLE TO A DEGREE.

27. Please indicate the terms in which you were enrolled for courses applicable to a degree. (CIRCLE AS MANY AS APPLY)

Summer, 1961 x   12
Fall semester or quarter, 1961 0   Y
Winter quarter, 1961–62 1
Spring semester or quarter, 1962 2

---

28. If you are not currently enrolled this spring term, which of the following best explains why you are not enrolled now? (CIRCLE ANY WHICH APPLY)

Have already received my postgraduate degree . . . . . . Y   13
Completed the course work for the degree x   R
Academic difficulties or fear of academic difficulties . . . 0
Lost interest 1
Required too much time 2
Decided to switch fields 3
Health, called up for military service, or other unforeseen
    personal obstacle 4
Financial costs 5
Moved from the city 6
Family responsibilities 7
Am doing independent research, completing thesis, etc. . 8
Other (CIRCLE AND SPECIFY) _____ 9

---

29. Which of the following best describes your current (most recent) study program? (CIRCLE ONE)

Studying in a program in which full-time study is possible
   and carrying
     full-time load or greater 5   14
     more than half, but less than full load 6   4
     half a course load or less 7

Studying in a night school, or similar program in which
"full-time study" is impossible 8
Taking a correspondence course 9

---

30. Write the code number from the cover page which best describes:

A. Your current (most recent) field of study.

$$\frac{15-16}{\text{x}\quad\text{x}}$$

☐☐

B. Did you apply for graduate or professional (post-bachelor) studies in any other field prior to beginning study in your current (most recent) field?

No (WRITE "YY" IN THE
   BOXES)
Yes (INDICATE FIELD) $\dfrac{17-18}{\text{x}\quad\text{x}}$

☐☐

C. Do you plan to get a degree in any field other than the one in which you have been studying?

No (WRITE "YY" IN THE
   BOXES)
Yes (INDICATE FIELD) $\dfrac{19-20}{\text{x}\quad\text{x}}$

☐☐

IF YES: What are your reasons for changing? _____
_____

---

31. Please write the name of the school which you are now attending or have most recently attended since receiving your bachelor's degree.

School	City	State (Country If Non-U.S.)

32. Compared with the school where you completed your undergraduate work, is your current (last) school (CIRCLE ONE)

The same institution . . . . x $\dfrac{21}{\text{Y}}$
A different institution
    in the same city or within communting distance 0
    within four hours' automobile drive or less 1
    more than four hours' drive 2

---

33. Which of the following reasons played a part in your decision to attend this school rather than some other? (CIRCLE ANY WHICH APPLY)

Couldn't be admitted to one or more schools which I
    would have preferred . . . . Y   22
Cheaper tuition X   R̄
Offered more (some) financial aid by this school 0
Course work appeared easier . . . . '. . 1
Reputation and quality of University as a whole 2
Reputation and quality of my department or professional
    school 3
Allowed part-time or evening courses 4
Within commuting distance of my home or job 5
Course offerings more suited to my needs 6
Job opportunities for myself (or spouse) while in school . 7
Attracted to community or area in which school is
    situated 8
Sent here by my employer 9
Other (CIRCLE AND SPECIFY) ———————————— R

---

34. What is your grade point average so far in your post-bachelor's studies? If letter grades are not given, translate into letter grades as best you can. (CIRCLE ONE)

                                   A 0   23
                                   A − 1   Ȳ
                                   B+ 2
                                   B 3
                                   B − 4
                                   C+ 5
                                   C 6
                                   C − 7
                                   Less than C − 8
                                   No grades received yet . x

---

35. For each of the following three aspects of your post-bachelor's studies please indicate both the expectations you had before you began studying at this level and your experiences since you have been studying at this level. (CIRCLE ONE NUMBER ON EACH LINE)

Expectation and Experience	Aspect	Very	Fairly	Neither	Fairly	Very	Aspect
I expected to find course work	Hard	x	0	1	2	3	Easy
work load taking	Large share of my time	x	0	1	2	3	Little time
course content	Fascinating	x	0	1	2	3	Dull
I actually found course work	Hard	5	6	7	8	9	Easy
work load taking	Large share of my time	5	6	7	8	9	Little time
course content	Fascinating	5	6	7	8	9	Dull

36. How would you rate the following aspects of your studies this year? (CIRCLE ONE ANSWER FOR EACH ASPECT)

Aspect	Excellent	Good	Average	Poor	Don't Know, Inapplicable	
Caliber of classroom teaching	x	0	1	2	3	30 / Y
Curriculum and course offerings	5	6	7	8	9	31 / 4
Facilities and opportunities for research (including library)	x	0	1	2	3	32 / Y
Student housing	5	6	7	8	9	33 / 4
Caliber of students	x	0	1	2	3	34 / Y
Knowledge and professional standing of the faculty	5	6	7	8	9	35 / 4
Personal contacts with faculty	x	0	1	2	3	36 / Y

37. During the time you have been studying this academic year (1961–62), which of the following will have provided you with $200 or more in financial support? (CIRCLE ANY WHICH APPLY)

Full-time job x   37
Subsidy from present or future employer 0   Y
Income from spouse's employment 1
Parents or relatives 2
Withdrawals from savings 3
National Defense Education Act loan 4
Other loan 5
Part-time job other than a research or teaching assistant-
ship 6
None of the above 7

---

38. During the academic year, did you receive a stipend (scholarship, fellowship, research or teaching assistantship) or similar financial aid to students?

> Exclude loans and gifts from parents or relatives.
> Include reduction in fees even if you do not receive the money directly.
> Consider work as a stipend if you are receiving income from teaching or research in your field of study and are paid by your school or an affiliated organization.

No (CIRCLE AND SKIP TO QUESTION 40) x   38
Yes (CIRCLE AND SEE INSTRUCTIONS) 0   Y

> IF YES: On the back of the cover letter is a set of code numbers that describe stipends by source and type. Use the code numbers to answer the following questions.

> A. Describe your stipend (if you have two or more, de-   39–40
>   scribe the one that has the highest value).   ☐☐   x   x

> B. Do you have a second stipend?

>   IF YES: Describe it.   41–42
>   IF NO: Write "YY" in the boxes.   ☐☐   x   x

---

39. Please estimate the total value you received from all stipends during the academic year 1961–62. Include in your estimate the value of a tuition scholarship, or tuition remission (even if you received no money),

income from teaching or research in your field if you were paid by your school or affiliated organization. (CIRCLE ONE)

Less than $200 1		43
$200 – $499 2		0
$500 – $999 3		
$1,000 – $1,499 4		
$1,500 – $1,999 5		
$2,000 – $2,499 6		
$2,500 – $2,999 7		
$3,000 – $3,999 8		
$4,000 and over 9		

PLANS FOR NEXT YEAR (1962 – 63)

On the back of the cover letter is a set of code numbers that describe stipends by source and type. Use the code numbers to answer the following questions.

40. A. Have you accepted any stipend for the academic year 1962 – 63?

    IF NO: Write "YY" in boxes and skip to B.
    IF YES: (1) Describe your stipend. (If you have two or more, describe the one that has the highest value.) $\underline{44-45}$ □□ x x

    (2) Do you have a second stipend?
    IF YES: Describe it. $\underline{46-47}$
    IF NO: Write "YY" in the boxes. □□ x x

    B. Did you decline any stipend that you were offered for the academic year 1962 – 63?

    IF NO: Write "YY" in the boxes.
    IF YES: Describe the stipend you were offered. (If you were offered more than one, describe the "best" one.) $\underline{48-49}$ □□ x x

    C. Did you apply for the academic year 1962 – 63 for any stipend that is still pending?

IF NO: Write "YY" in the boxes.
IF YES: Describe the stipend. (If more than one is 50–51
pending, describe the "best" one.) ☐☐ x   x

D. Did you apply for the academic year 1962–63 for any stipend
for which you were rejected?

IF NO: Write "YY" in the boxes.
IF YES: Describe the stipend. (If more than one rejec- 52–53
tion, describe the stipend you would have preferred.) ☐☐ x   x

41. Indicate your plans for the coming (1962–63) academic year, by
circling one of the following:

Will continue studies in
Same field, same school 2   54
*Same field, but different school 3   1
*Same school, but different field 4
*Different field and different school 5
Will not be enrolled because
Work for degree will be completed 6
Studying in absentia 7
*Interrupting my studies temporarily 8
*Quitting my studies short of the degree 9
*Why are you making the change or changes indicated
(*) above? _____

42. If you plan to go to school in the coming year, 1962–63, do you
plan to go (CIRCLE ONE)

Full time x   55
Part time 0   Y

43. Did getting (or not getting) a stipend influence your plans for
next year?

No (CIRCLE AND SKIP   56
TO QUESTION 49) . . 3   2
*Yes 4

*IF YES: What was the influence? _____

PLEASE SKIP TO QUESTION 49.

Answer the following questions if you have not been enrolled since
June, 1961, for courses applicable to a degree. (If you have been enrolled for such courses during the specified time period, skip to Question 49.)

44. A. Had you at any time considered enrolling during this current
(1961–62) school year for degree study (on campus or by correspondence)? (CIRCLE ONE)

No . . . . X BEGIN
*Considered it, but did not apply to any school . . . . . . 0 DECK 3
*Applied to one or more schools, was not accepted by
   any 1   11
*Applied to one or more schools, accepted by one or   Y
   more 2

---

*B. IF YOU CONSIDERED OR APPLIED: Write the code number from
   the cover page which best describes the field you considered.
                                               ☐☐   12–13
                                                      X   X

---

45. Which of the following describes your reasons for not enrolling
this past year? (CIRCLE AS MANY AS APPLY)

No desire to do so . . . . Y   14
Could get a desirable job without further schooling X   R
I wanted to get practical experience first 0
Finances 1
Fear of academic difficulties 2
Problem of admission to the school (type of school) I
   wished to attend 3
Military service, active duty or reserve program 4
Health or other personal obstacles 5
Family responsibilities 6
Lack of time 7
No school available where I was living 8
Other (CIRCLE AND SPECIFY) ————————— 9

---

46. Have you considered enrolling next year (any time between June,
1962, and June, 1963) for courses applicable to a degree (on campus or
by correspondence)?

No (CIRCLE AND SKIP TO QUESTION 48) 4   15
Yes (CIRCLE AND CONTINUE WITH QUESTION 47) 5   3

47. IF YOU CONSIDERED ENROLLING NEXT YEAR

   A. Have you applied for admission to any school for the coming
   year (1962–63)? (CIRCLE ONE)

No, and I'm not planning to apply this year (CIRCLE

AND SKIP TO D) 0

No, but I'm still planning to apply (CIRCLE AND SKIP TO

B) 1

*Yes, I applied to one school 2

*Yes, I applied to two or three schools 3

*Yes, I applied to four or more schools 4

16
R

   *IF YOU'VE APPLIED: (1) What is the current status of your ap-
   plications? (CIRCLE ONE IN EACH COLUMN)

Number of Schools	Accepted By: (Circle One)	Rejected By: (Circle One)	Pending At: (Circle One)
No schools	5	5	5
One school	6	6	6
Two or three schools	7	7	7
Four or more schools	8	8	8
	17	18	19
	R	R	R

On the back of the cover letter is a set of code numbers that describe
stipends by source and type. Use the code numbers to answer the following questions.

   B. (1) Have you accepted any stipend (scholarship, fellowship,
      research or teaching assistantship) or similar financial
      aid to students, for the academic year 1962–63?

Exclude loans and gifts from parents or relatives.

Include reduction in fees, even if you do not receive the money
   directly.

Consider work as a stipend, if you are receiving income from
   teaching or research in your field of study and are paid by your
   school or an affiliated organization.

IF NO: Write "YY" in the boxes and skip to (2).

IF YES: (a) Describe your stipend. (If you have two or more,
   describe the one that has the highest value.)

20–21
☐☐ R R

(*b*) Do you have a second stipend?

IF YES: Describe it.

IF NO: Write "YY" in the boxes.

22 – 23

☐☐ R   R

    (2) Did you decline any stipend that you were offered for the academic year 1962 – 63?

IF NO: Write "YY" in the boxes.

IF YES: Describe the stipend you declined. (If you declined more than one, describe the "best" one.)

24 – 25

☐☐ R   R

    (3) Did you apply for any stipend for the academic year 1962 – 63, that is still pending?

IF NO: Write "YY" in the boxes.

IF YES: Describe the stipend. (If more than one is pending, describe the "best" one.)

26 – 27

☐☐ R   R

    (4) Did you apply for any stipend for the academic year 1962 – 63 for which you were rejected?

IF NO: Write "YY" in the boxes.

IF YES: Describe the stipend. (If more than one rejection, describe the stipend you would have preferred.)

28 – 29

☐☐ R   R

C. Did getting (or not getting) a stipend influence your plans for next year?

No 0

Yes 1

30

R

D. Do you expect to enroll for further degree study during the coming academic year (1962 – 63) either on campus or by correspondence?

No (CIRCLE AND ANSWER QUESTION 48) 6

*Yes, on campus full time 7

*Yes, on campus part time 8

*Yes, correspondence 9

31

R

*What are you planning to study? (Indicate the field by copying the code numbers from list inside the cover letter.)

32 – 33

☐☐ R   R

SKIP TO QUESTION 49.

---

48. FOR THOSE NOT PLANNING TO BE ENROLLED DURING THE COMING ACADEMIC YEAR (1962 – 63).

A. Do you expect to go on for further degree study (on campus or by correspondence) in the future? (CIRCLE ONE)

No (CIRCLE AND SKIP TO QUESTION 49) . . . . 0 $\frac{34}{R}$
Probably not (CIRCLE AND SKIP TO QUESTION 49) 1
*Probably yes 2
*Yes 3

*IF YES OR PROBABLY YES:

(1) When do you expect to begin? Make your single best prediction (CIRCLE ONE)

Academic year
1963 – 64 . . . . 5 $\frac{35}{R}$
1964 – 65 6
1965 – 66 7
1966 – 67 8
No specific date in
mind 9

(2) Refer to the field list and write the code number which best describes the field in which you expect to study. $\frac{36-37}{R \quad R}$

(3) Which of the following best explains why you are postponing your further studies? (CIRCLE ANY WHICH APPLY)

I want to get practical experience first . . . . 2 $\frac{38}{R}$
Finances 3
Military service, active duty or reserve program 4
Problem of getting admitted 5
Health or other personal obstacle 6
Family responsibilities 7
No school available where I am now living 8
Other (CIRCLE AND SPECIFY) ——————————————

ATTITUDES AND OPINIONS

EVERYBODY PLEASE ANSWER:

49. How would you rate the following aspects of your undergraduate college or university? (CIRCLE ONE ANSWER FOR EACH ASPECT)

Lawyers in the Making

Aspect	Excellent	Good	Average	Poor	Don't Know or Inapplicable	
Caliber of classroom teaching	x	0	1	2	3	39/Y
Curriculum and course offerings	5	6	7	8	9	40/4
Facilities and opportunities for research (including library)	x	0	1	2	3	41/Y
Student housing	5	6	7	8	9	42/4
Caliber of the students	x	0	1	2	3	43/Y
Knowledge and professional standing of the faculty	5	6	7	8	9	44/4

50. During the year since you graduated, have any of the following been a source of worry or concern for you? (CIRCLE AS MANY AS APPLY)

My children's health and development 1   45/0
Ability to make friends 2
Physical health 3
Finances 4
Loneliness 5
Dating, relations with opposite sex 6
Goals in life 7
Relations with spouse 8

Career plans 1   46/0
School studies this year 2
Emotional state 3
Relations with my parents 4
World conditions 5
Relations with in-laws 6
My job 7
Other problems (CIRCLE AND SPECIFY) _____ 8
None, no worries 9

51. Which of the following do you expect to give you the most satisfaction in your life?

Activity	Most Satisfaction (Circle One)	Next Most Satisfaction (Circle One)
Your career or occupation	x	x
Family relationships	0	0
Leisure-time recreational activities	1	1
Religious beliefs or activities	2	2
Participation as a citizen in the affairs of your community	3	3
Participation in activities directed toward national or international betterment	4	4

	47	48
	Y	Y

52. Listed below are some adjectives, some of which are "favorable," some of which are "unfavorable," some of which are neither. (PLEASE CIRCLE THE ONES WHICH BEST DESCRIBE YOU.) Consider only those which are most characteristic of you as a person. (Most people choose five or six, but you may choose more or fewer if you want to.)

Ambitious 0	Energetic 0
Athletic 1	Fun loving 1
Calm 2	Good looking 2
Cautious 3	Happy 3
Conventional 4	Hard driving 4
Cooperative 5	High strung 5
Cultured 6	Idealistic 6
Dominant 7	Impetuous 7
Easy going 8	Intellectual 8
Efficient 9	Lazy 9

49 R   50 R

Methodical 0	Quiet 0
Middle brow 1	Rebellious 1
Moody 2	Religious 2
Nervous 3	Reserved 3
Non-religious 4	Shy 4
Obliging 5	Sophisticated 5
Outgoing 6	Talkative 6
Poised 7	Tense 7
Politically liberal 8	Unconventional 8
Politically conservative . . . 9	Witty 9

51 R   52 R

53. How would you feel about working overseas for a few years, in your regular occupation, for each of the following types of organization? (CIRCLE ONE FOR EACH KIND OF ORGANIZATION)

Feeling	Private Business (Circle One)	Non-Profit Organization (Circle One)	Federal Government Agency (Circle One)	U.N. or Other International Agencies (Circle One)
Definitely would like to	x	3	7	x
Would like to under certain conditions	0	4	8	0
Definitely would not like to	1	5	9	1
	$\frac{53}{Y}$	$\frac{54}{2}$	$\frac{55}{6}$	$\frac{56}{Y}$

54. A. Since you began college, have you seriously considered employment in any of the following federal governmental departments or agencies or in the Peace Corps? (CIRCLE ANY WHICH APPLY)

IF NO: CIRCLE AND SKIP TO QUESTION 55 . . . . x $\frac{57}{Y}$

IF YES: INDICATE WHICH AGENCY(IES)

State Department 0
United States Information Agency 1
Central Intelligence Agency 2
Agency for International Development (formerly
  I.C.A.) 3
Peace Corps 4
Other in international affairs (CIRCLE AND SPECIFY) _____ 5

Agriculture . . . . x $\frac{58}{R}$
Commerce (includes Census) 0
Federal Reserve Board 1
Health, Education, and Welfare 2
Interior 3
Justice (includes FBI) 4
Labor (includes BLS) 5
Defense (includes career military service) 6
Post Office 7
Treasury (includes internal revenue) 8
Other in domestic fields (CIRCLE AND SPECIFY) _____ 9

B. Have you taken any of the following federal governmental examinations? (CIRCLE ONE OR MORE OF THE ALTERNATIVES FOR EACH OF THE EXAMINATIONS)

Examination Status	Peace Corps (PC) (Circle One or More)	Federal Service Entrance (FSEE) (Circle One or More)	Management Interne (MI) (Circle One or More)	Foreign Service Officers (FSO) (Circle One or More)	United States Information Agency (USIA) (Circle One or More)
I have taken it	0	0	0	0	0
I took it and plan to take it again	1	1	1	1	1
I haven't taken it but plan to do so	2	2	2	2	2
I never heard of the exam	3	3	3	3	3
I've heard of it but have decided not to to take it because:					
I don't think I could pass the exam	4	4	4	4	4
Even if I passed the exam I probably wouldn't be selected	5	5	5	5	5
I wouldn't like to be subjected to the investigation involved	6	6	6	6	6
It takes too long to find out whether you're selected	7	7	7	7	7
I'm not interested in the types of governmental positions filled through this exam	8	8	8	8	8
Other (CIRCLE AND SPECIFY)	9	9	9	9	9
	$\frac{59}{R}$	$\frac{60}{R}$	$\frac{61}{R}$	$\frac{62}{R}$	$\frac{63}{R}$

FINANCES

55. Considering money borrowed for education (tuition, living expenses while in school, books, etc.), how much money	None	Less Than $500	$500 to $999	$1,000 or More	
A. do you personally owe now for undergraduate training? (CIRCLE ONE)	6	7	8	9	$\frac{64}{5}$
B. have you borrowed for postgraduate studies? (CIRCLE ONE)	6	7	8	9	$\frac{65}{5}$
C. do you expect to borrow for postgraduate studies next year (academic year 1962–63)? (CIRCLE ONE)	6	7	8	9	$\frac{66}{5}$

56. How much do you have in the form of savings and securities (or other assets which could be converted into cash in an emergency) and how much are you currently in debt (excluding mortgages, bills paid within the month, etc.)?

Indebtedness	Assets (Circle One)	Debts and Liabilities (Circle One)
Nothing	x	x
Less than $199	0	0
$100–$499	1	1
$500–$999	2	2
$1,000–$4,999	3	3
$5,000 or more	4	4
	$\frac{67}{Y}$	$\frac{68}{Y}$

57. Please estimate your current average monthly income before taxes and deductions. Do not include any income you may have from scholarships, assistantships, or other stipends awarded to students. (CIRCLE ONE IN EACH COLUMN)

Monthly Income	From Your Own Employment (Circle One)	Total Monthly Income (Including Spouse's and Other Income) (Circle One)	What Do You Regard as an Adequate Monthly Income for a Person in Your Circumstances? (Circle One)
None	2	2	2
$1–$199	3	3	3
$200–$299	4	4	4
$300–$399	5	5	5
$400–$599	6	6	6
$600–$799	7	7	7
$800–$999	8	8	8
$1,000 or more	9	9	9
	$\frac{69}{1}$	$\frac{70}{1}$	$\frac{71}{1}$

58. How many of your grandparents were born in the United States? (CIRCLE ONE)

$$
\begin{array}{ll}
\text{None} \dots\dots\dots 0 & \dfrac{72}{x} \\
\text{One} \dots\dots\dots 1 & \\
\text{Two} \dots\dots\dots 2 & \\
\text{Three} \dots\dots\dots 3 & \\
\text{Four} \dots\dots\dots 4 &
\end{array}
$$

59. What is your predominant national background?	Mother's Side of Family (Circle One)	Father's Side of Family (Circle One)
English, Scotch, Welsh, English-Canadian, Australian, New Zealand	x	x
Irish	0	0
German, Austrian, Swiss	1	1
Scandinavian	2	2
Italian	3	3
French, French-Canadian, Belgian	4	4
Polish	5	5
Russian and other Eastern European	6	6
American Negro	7	7
Spanish, Portuguese, and Latin American (Mexican, Puerto Rican, Central and South American)	8	8
Other (CIRCLE AND SPECIFY)	9	9
	$\frac{73}{Y}$	$\frac{74}{Y}$

60. How frequently do you attend religious services? (CIRCLE THE CLOSEST NUMBER)

Weekly, almost without exception . . . . 4 $\frac{75}{3}$
Several times a month 5
Once a month 6
Two or three times a year 7
Once a year 8
Never 9

A. In the box at the bottom of the page is your current mailing address, according to our records.

If it is correct, circle the letter x to the right x
If not, please circle the letter y to the right and make any necessary correction . . . . Y

We will use this address to mail you a copy of a report on our research as soon as we receive your questionnaire.

B. Is this (corrected) current address your most likely address one year from now?

Yes 1
*No 2

*IF NO: Your most likely address one year from now

Name of residence hall, department, company, etc., if any

Street address

City or town   Zone   State or country

EVERYBODY ANSWER

C. Name and address of someone who will know where you are or could forward a letter to you if you were not at the address you listed above:

_____

First name   Middle name   Last name

_____

_____

Street address

_____

_____

City or town   Zone   State or country

_____

IMPORTANT

You have now completed the questionnaire. Please drop it in the enclosed postage paid envelope and return it to us.

Thank you very much and good luck.

References

Barton, A. H., and Lazarsfeld, P. F. *Methodology of quantitative social research.* Bureau of Applied Social Research, Columbia University. Publication No. A–349. Reprinted from B. N. Varma (Ed.), *A new survey of the social sciences.* New York: Asia Publishing House, 1962. Pp. 151–68.

Berelson, B. Graduate education in the United States. New York: McGraw-Hill, 1960.

Carlin, J. E. *Current research in the sociology of the legal profession.* Bureau of Applied Social Research, Columbia University, 1962. Mimeographed. (a)

――――. *Lawyers on their own.* New Brunswick, N.J.: Rutgers University Press, 1962. (b)

Davies, V. *Rapid method for determining significance of the difference between two percentages.* Washington State University, Washington Agricultural Experiment Stations, Institute of Agricultural Sciences, July, 1962.

Davis, J. A. *Great aspirations.* Chicago: Aldine Publishing Co., 1964.

――――. *Undergraduate career decisions.* Chicago: Aldine Publishing Co., 1965.

Fauman, S. J. Occupational selection among Detroit Jews. In M. Sklare (Ed.), *The Jews: Social patterns of an American group.* Glencoe, Ill.: Free Press, 1958. Pp. 119–37.

Festinger, L. *A theory of cognitive dissonance.* Stanford, Calif.: Stanford University Press, 1957.

Goldberg, D., and Sharp, H. Some characteristics of Detroit area Jewish and non-Jewish adults. In M. Sklare (Ed.), *The Jews: Social patterns of an American group.* Glencoe, Ill.: Free Press, 1958. Pp. 107–18.

Greeley, A. M. *Religion and career: A study of college graduates.* New York: Sheed and Ward, 1963.

Hodge, R., Siegel, P. M., and Rossi, P. H. Occupational prestige in the United States, 1925–63. *Amer. J. Sociol.,* 1964, **70**, 286–302.

Kendall, P., and Lazarsfeld, P. F. Problems of survey analysis. In R. K. Merton and P. F. Lazarsfeld (Eds.), *Continuities in social research: Studies in the scope and method of "The American soldier."* Glencoe, Ill.: Free Press, 1950. Pp. 133–96.

Ladinsky, J. Careers of lawyers, law practice, and legal institutions. *Amer. sociol. Rev.,* 1963, **28**, 47–54.

Lortie, D. C. The striving young lawyer. Unpublished doctoral dissertation, Department of Sociology, University of Chicago, 1958.

Miller, N. *One year after commencement: An interim report on the 1961–62 graduate school enrollment and the future career plans of the 1961–62 college graduating class.* National Opinion Research Center, 1963. Report No. 93. Multilithed.

Rogoff, N. Recent trends in occupational mobility. Unpublished doctoral dissertation, University of Chicago, 1950.

Smigel, E. O. The impact of recruitment on the organization of the large law firm. *Amer. sociol. Rev.,* 1960, **25**, 56–66.

――――. The Wall Street lawyer. New York: The Free Press of Glencoe, 1964.

STRODTBECK, F. L. Family interaction, values, and achievement. In D. C. MCCLELLAND *et al.* (Eds.), *Talent and society.* Princeton, N.J.: D. Van Nostrand Co., 1958. Pp. 135–94.

U.S. DEPARTMENT OF COMMERCE, BUREAU OF THE CENSUS. *U.S. census of population: 1960. Subject reports. Occupational Characteristics. Final report PC(2)-7A.* Washington, D.C.: U.S. Government Printing Office, 1963.

WINTERBOTTOM, J. A., and JOHNSON, A. P. *The law school admissions test program.* Princeton, N.J.: Educational Testing Service, September, 1961. Lithographed.

Index

Academic Performance Index (API): and career preference, 8–9, 45, *1.8*, *3.3*; definition of, 8; and entry into law school and career preference, 38–41, *2.12*; and entry into law school and father's education, 37–38, *2.11*; and entry into law school and parental income, 37, *2.9*; and entry into law school and parental occupation, 37–38, *2.10*; and entry into law school and plans for graduate or professional study, 30–31, *2.3*; and entry into law school and reasons for not applying for a stipend, 83, *6.2*, *6.3*; and entry into law school and religious origin, 36–37, *2.8*; and entry into law school and stipend application, 81–83, *6.1*; and Law School Admission Test status, 15, *1.14a*; and law-school grades, 75–76, *5.5*; and law-school stratum, 55, 65–67, *4.2*, *5.2a*; and law-school stratum and expected work setting, 108–9, *7.6*; and law-school stratum and father's education, 57–58, *4.4*; and law-school stratum and law-school course-load, 69–70, *5.3*; and law-school stratum and law-school grades, 76–78, *5.6*; and law-school stratum and parental income, 55–58, *4.3*; and law-school stratum and reactions to first year of law school, 70–75, *5.4*; and law-school stratum and religious origin, 58–59, *4.5*; and law-school stratum and stipend holding, 83–87, *6.4*; and law-school stratum, stipend holding, and parental income, 87–88, *6.5*; and law-school Stratum I, religious origin, and metropolitan origin, 59–60, *4.6*; and parental occupation and career preference, 45–47, *3.4*; and parental

occupation, career preference, and religious origin, 47–49, *3.6*, *3.7*
Age and Law School Admission Test status, 15, *1.13f*
Anticipated career employer and career preference, 12–13, *1.11*

Berelson, B., 55*n*
Bradburn, N.: *see* Davis, J. A.

Career preference: and Academic Performance Index, 45, *3.3*; and anticipated career employer, 12–13, *1.11*; and change and stability in choice, 1–2, 3–6, 38–41, *1.1*; and entry into law school and Academic Performance Index, 38–41, *2.12*; and father's education, 3, *1.4*; and Law School Admission Test score, 25, *1.19*; and Law School Admission Test status, 14, *1.12*; and mother's education, 3, *1.5*; and occupational values, 10–12, *1.10*; and parental income, 3, *1.3*; and parental occupation, 3, 43, *1.2*, *3.1*; and parental occupation and Academic Performance Index, 45–47, *3.4*; and parental occupation, Academic Performance Index, and religious origin, 47–49, *3.6*, *3.7*; and parental occupation and religious origin, 45–46, *3.5*; and plans for graduate or professional study, 28, *2.1*; and religious origin, 45, *3.3*; and size of community, 7, *1.7*; and socio-economic status, 44–45, 62–63, *3.2*; and undergraduate school, 9–10, *1.9*
Carlin, J. E., 63, 64
Census, 1960: and income rank of lawyers and judges, 50*n*
Continuation of legal studies: and law-school stratum and law-school grades, 100–102, *7.1*

NOTE: numerals in *italics* are table numbers.